Enacting and Conceptualizing Educational Leadership within the Mediterranean Region

Comparative Education and the Mediterranean Region

Series Editor

Ronald G. Sultana (*University of Malta*)

Editorial Board

Abdeljalil Akkari (*University of Geneva, Switzerland*)
Rima Karami Akkary (*American University of Beirut, Lebanon*)
Xavier Bonal i Sarró (*Autonomous University of Barcelona, Spain*)
Hülya Kosar-Altinyelken (*University of Amsterdam, the Netherlands*)
Paolo Landri (*National Research Council, Italy*)
António Magalhães (*University of Porto, Portugal*)
André E. Mazawi (*University of British Columbia, Canada*)
Nagwa Megahed (*Ain Shams University, Egypt*)
Michalinos Zembylas (*Open University of Cyprus, Cyprus*)

VOLUME 2

The titles published in this series are listed at *brill.com/mena*

Enacting and Conceptualizing Educational Leadership within the Mediterranean Region

Edited by

Denise Mifsud and Paolo Landri

BRILL
SENSE

LEIDEN | BOSTON

All chapters in this book have undergone peer review.

The Library of Congress Cataloging-in-Publication Data is available online at http://catalog.loc.gov

Typeface for the Latin, Greek, and Cyrillic scripts: "Brill". See and download: brill.com/brill-typeface.

ISSN 2667-0046
ISBN 978-90-04-46185-7 (paperback)
ISBN 978-90-04-46186-4 (hardback)
ISBN 978-90-04-46187-1 (e-book)

Copyright 2021 by Koninklijke Brill NV, Leiden, The Netherlands.
Koninklijke Brill NV incorporates the imprints Brill, Brill Hes & De Graaf, Brill Nijhoff, Brill Rodopi, Brill Sense, Hotei Publishing, mentis Verlag, Verlag Ferdinand Schöningh and Wilhelm Fink Verlag.
All rights reserved. No part of this publication may be reproduced, translated, stored in a retrieval system, or transmitted in any form or by any means, electronic, mechanical, photocopying, recording or otherwise, without prior written permission from the publisher. Requests for re-use and/or translations must be addressed to Koninklijke Brill NV via brill.com or copyright.com.

This book is printed on acid-free paper and produced in a sustainable manner.

Contents

Notes on Contributors VII

1 Problematizing the Dominant Discourses and Policies of Educational Leadership within the Mediterranean Basin 1
    Denise Mifsud and Paolo Landri

2 Social Justice and Education in the Maltese State School System: Some Political and Practical Issues 11
    Denise Mifsud

3 Challenges to Educational Leadership in Israel 37
    Devorah Kalekin-Fishman

4 The New Public Governance: Corporate Leadership in Spain's Public Education System 62
    Enrique-Javier Díez-Gutiérrez

5 School Leadership within a Centralized Education System: A Success Story from Cyprus through a Decade of Research 79
    Petros Pashiardis and Antonios Kafa

6 Educational Leadership in Algeria: A Decisive Factor in the 2004 Higher Education Reform 101
    Mohamed Miliani

7 Digitally Equipped: Reshaping Educational Leadership and Management in Italy 117
    Paolo Landri and Danilo Taglietti

8 How Do Portuguese Principals Deal with Competing Demands? Issues of Bureaucracy, Performativity and Democracy 135
    Maria Assunção Flores and Fernando Ilídio Ferreira

Index 161

Notes on Contributors

Enrique-Javier Díez-Gutiérrez
is Full Professor at the University of León's Education Faculty (Spain). Educational organization specialist. Currently performing his teaching and research tasks in the field of Intercultural Education, gender, and education policy. He has worked as a social educator, as a primary school teacher, as a secondary school teacher, as a guidance counselor in high schools and as a person responsible for attention to diversity in the Spanish educational administration for more than 20 years. Latest publications are: *La asignatura pendiente* (*The Pending Subject*) (Plaza y Valdés, 2020); *La educación en venta* (*Education for Sale*) (Octaedro, 2020); *Educación para el bien común* (*Education for the Common Good*) (Octaedro, 2020) with Juan Ramón Rodríguez; *La Polis Secuestrada* (*The Kidnapped Polis*) (Trea, 2019) with Juan Ramón Rodríguez; and *Neoliberalismo educativo* (*Educational Neoliberalism*) (Octaedro, 2018).

Fernando Ilídio Ferreira
is Associate Professor at the University of Minho, Portugal where he received his PhD in Child Studies. He teaches Sociology of Education, Education Policies, Intercultural Education, Educational Practicum in Preschool and Primary School, amongst others. His research interests include teacher education, leadership, continuing education, community development, early childhood and primary education, childhood studies and children's rights.

Maria Assunção Flores
is Associate Professor with qualification at the University of Minho, Portugal. She received her PhD at the University of Nottingham, UK. Her research interests include teacher professionalism and identity, teacher education and professional development, teacher appraisal, curriculum, assessment, leadership and higher education. She has published extensively on these topics both nationally and internationally. She was Chair of the International Study Association on Teachers and Teaching (ISATT) between 2013 and 2019. She is co-editor of the *European Journal of Teacher Education*.

Antonios Kafa
holds a PhD in Educational Leadership and Policy from the Open University of Cyprus. Currently, he is working at Frederick University, in the MA study programme Educational Administration. He holds a BA in Philosophy, Education and Psychology from the University of Athens and an MA in Educational Leadership from the European University Cyprus. His doctoral dissertation was

awarded a "Highly Commended Award Winner" – Emerald/EFMD Outstanding Doctoral Research Awards 2016, in the Educational leadership and strategy field. He is also participating as a member in the international comparative research project entitled "International Successful School Principalship Project" (ISSPP). Furthermore, he is one of the members of the Board of Directors of the Cyprus Educational Administration Society, as well as a lecturer at the Cyprus Police Academy. He authored a number of papers in peer-reviewed journals and participates in various European and international conferences. His research interests include different aspects of educational administration such as successful school leadership and school principals' personal values systems.

Devorah Kalekin-Fishman
is a Senior Researcher in the Faculty of Education, the University of Haifa. She has published widely on alienation, the sociology of everyday life, the sociology of knowledge, sociology of the senses, and problems in education. Authored and edited books include: *Ideology, Policy and Practice* (Kluwer, 2003), *Radicals in Spite of Themselves* (with Schneider, Sense, 2007), *From the Margins to New Ground* (with L. Hagoel, Sense, 2016), *Practicing Social Science* (Routledge, 2017), *Alienation and the Millennium* (with L. Langman, Krieger, 1996), *Multiple Citizenship in Europe* (with P. Pitkanen, Peter Lang, 2007), *The ISA Handbook in Contemporary Sociology* (with A. Denis, Sage, 2009), *Everyday Life in Asia* (with K. Low, Routledge, 2010), *The Shape of Sociology for the 21st Century.* (with A. Denis, Sage, 2012), *Approaches to Educational and Social Inclusion: An International Perspective* (with G. K. Verma, Routledge, 2016). Currently, she is involved in a study of the implementation of her model for 'Acquiring Literacy in Participatory Citizenship' (with L. Hagoel, submitted). She serves on the editorial boards of several international journals, is associate editor of *Sociopedia,* and was Vice-President for Publications in the International Sociological Association (2006-2010).

Paolo Landri
is a Senior Researcher of the Institute of Research on Population and Social Policies at National Research Council in Italy (CNR-IRPPS). His main research interests concern educational organizations, digital governance and educational policies. His latest publication is *Educational Leadership, Management, and Administration through Actor Network Theory* (Routledge, 2020).

Denise Mifsud
is the Head of College Network, providing leadership to the thirteen state primary and secondary schools in Gozo. Besides this, she is an independent education researcher and consultant, with many years of practitioner experience

in education settings in both teaching and leadership roles. She previously held a full-time lecturing post at the University of the West of Scotland as well as being a part-time lecturer at the University of Malta. She is also an Associate Fellow of the Euro-Mediterranean Centre for Educational Research within the same university. She was awarded her PhD by the University of Stirling in 2015. Research areas of interest include educational policy analysis, generation, reception and enactment; leadership theories, with a particular interest in educational leadership, especially distributed forms; school networks and educational reform; initial teacher education; power relations; Foucauldian theory; Actor-Network Theory, as well as qualitative research methods, with a particular focus on narrative, as well as creative and unconventional modes of data representation. She has presented her research at various international conferences, besides winning numerous academic awards. She is a member of several professional organizations, in addition to being an Associate Fellow of the Higher Education Academy. She has published in several international top-rated journals, in addition to monographs and edited volumes.

Mohamed Miliani
is Professor of English at the University of Oran 2. He holds a BA in English, a Diploma in TEFL, an MEd, and a PhD from the University of Wales. He has been teaching at the University of Oran since 1974. He specializes in education, TEFL, and ESP. His research interests include sociolinguistics; Education/Training; TEFL; and language in education. He published articles in these areas. He has contributed to a number of book chapters (about preschooling, languages in education, evaluation of education system). He is research project leader in university ethics at the Centre de Recherche en Anthropologie Sociale et Culturelle, CRASC; Vice-president of the National Evaluation Committee (MOHE); Member of the Scientific Committee (National Institute for Research in Education, MNE); President of the Algerian Technical Committee for Education (UNESCO). He is HERE (Higher Education Reform Expert, Erasmus+ programme). He is Associate Fellow at Euro-Med Centre for Educational Research.

Petros Pashiardis
is a Professor of Educational Leadership and the Dean of the Faculty of Economics and Management at the Open University of Cyprus. He has also been a Visiting Professor with the University of Pretoria in South Africa, and a Visiting Scholar at the University of Stellenbosch, South Africa, as well as a Visiting Professor at the Centre for Principal Development, Umeå University, Sweden. For the period 2004-2008, Professor Pashiardis was President of the Commonwealth Council for Educational Administration and Management (CCEAM).

In 2014, his book *Modeling School Leadership across Europe: In Search of New Frontiers* was published by Springer Publications. His latest book in English (together with Olof Johansson) was published by Bloomsbury Publications in 2016, under the title: *Successful School Leadership: International Perspectives*. His research interests revolve around School Leadership as related to Pedagogical and Entrepreneurial Leadership; Leadership Effects and School Effectiveness; and Comparative/International Aspects of Educational Leadership. His current thinking takes him beyond the WHAT effective/successful school leaders do and into the HOW they do it, by re-examining ancient Greek philosophers as they relate to 21st century thinking and research on educational leadership.

Danilo Taglietti
is a PhD student in Social Sciences and Statistics, the University of Naples Federico II, Italy. He is interested in Education Policy Sociology and in the debate between modern and post-modern perspectives in sociological analysis. In his works, he tries to explore the actual shapes of the constitution of educational subjectivities at the crossroads of the complex entanglement among the forces of the informational, the biological and the economical. He adopts quantitative and qualitative approaches to address the problem of the reforming of educational systems and organizations not in terms of neoliberalism as a driving ideology or discourse, but in terms of the becoming neoliberal of our subjectivities.

CHAPTER 1

Problematizing the Dominant Discourses and Policies of Educational Leadership within the Mediterranean Basin

Denise Mifsud and Paolo Landri

Abstract

This introductory chapter sets the stage for this edited book that documents and deconstructs the concept of educational leadership within various education settings across the Mediterranean region, exploring the intersection of education, culture and geopolitics as shaped by the distinct social, religious, national, cultural and geographic contexts. Notoriously little agreement exists about how leadership may be defined – Alvesson and Spicer (2012) describe the field as characterized by 'conceptual confusion and endemic vagueness' (p. 369). This chapter problematizes the romanticization of leadership, as well as the concept of leader centrism, while deconstructing the search for a blueprint of competences that define leadership as an exceptional practice that can simply be simulated across situations, contexts and cultures. The authors further problematize the notions of universality and cultural contingency in educational leadership, given the recent unfolding of a cultural turn in educational leadership studies (Wilkinson & Bristol, 2018). Consequently, this chapter paves the way for the presentation of an understanding of the effect of state policies, geopolitics and popular culture on leadership enactment within the diverse education landscapes constituting the Mediterranean basin.

Key words

cultural contingency – deconstruction of leadership – educational leadership – globalization – leadership discourses – the Mediterranean Basin – universality

This volume documents and deconstructs the concept of educational leadership within various education settings across the Mediterranean region, exploring the intersection of education, culture and geopolitics as shaped by the distinct social, religious, national, cultural and geographic contexts. Notoriously little agreement exists about how leadership may be defined – Alvesson and Spicer (2012) describe the field as characterized by 'conceptual confusion and endemic vagueness' (p. 369). Ladkin (2010) celebrates this lack of definitional clarity, while inviting us 'to consider the very indefinability of leadership as significant' (p. 2), with each expression of leadership contributing to our understanding of its identity – the total determination of which remains elusive. Consequently, this volume seeks to present an understanding of the effect of state policies, geopolitics and popular culture on leadership enactment within the diverse education landscapes constituting the Mediterranean basin.

Alvesson and Spicer (2011) state that: 'The leader has become one of the dominant heroes of our time ... Whatever the problem, leadership has become the solution' (p. 1). We now live in a 'leadership-obsessed culture', a world dominated by the idea that leadership is one of the major factors – sometimes the only determining factor – of the success or otherwise of an educational organization. It is a society that according to Alvesson and Spicer (2012) practises a 'blind faith in the curative powers of leadership', while extolling its' celebration and naturalization' (p. 368), pushing us to deny 'ambiguities, incoherencies, and shifts in our great leaders' (ibid., 2011, p. 3). An outcome of society's love affair with leadership is what Fairhurst (2011) describes as 'leader centrism' (p. 190) – a tendency to focus primarily on leaders' actions, as well as the often unchallenged assumption of leadership as a positive thing, reflecting broader social beliefs in the power of the heroic individual, therefore manifesting a preference for the avoidance of what Festinger (1957) terms as 'cognitive dissonance'.

Wood and Case (2006) suggest that studies of leadership have been dominated by the search for a blueprint of competences, capabilities and models that can be implemented to achieve similar results. The existing frameworks of leadership construct it as something existing as an 'exceptional practice', resulting in a normalizing of leadership into models dominated by stories of heroic endeavours (Niesche, 2011, p. 2). This idealized concept of leadership is deconstructed by Christie and Lingard (2001), for whom leadership is 'a dynamic process where forces that are conscious and unconscious, rational and irrational, play out in complex social situations' (p. 138), thus doing away with any notion of heroism. Dickson et al. (2012) review the literature on the relationships between cultural dimensions and leadership, providing an overview of how the meaning of leadership varies systematically across cultures while drawing attention to the conflict in the literature between the quest for universals and the identification of cultural contingencies in leadership theory. They argue that, 'Viewed from a level of abstraction, there are aspects of leadership that appear to be universal across cultures ... But ... culture does matter, and not in a small way. It matters in how leaders emerge, are selected, developed, and seen (or not seen) as role models to be emulated, and it matters in ways that are predictable, and that organizations can respond to strategically' (p. 491). Moreover, they problematize the notions of 'universality' and 'cultural contingency' in the leadership concept. This problematization espouses three main issues that revolve around levels of analysis, cross-cultural leadership, and the North American 'flavour' of most cross-cultural leadership research. In order for conclusions to be reached about a specific phenomenon across cultures, studies have to be conducted at the individual, organizational, and national level, that is, at the micro, meso and macro strata. Leadership perceptions in different cultures impinge on the impact that culture has on leadership. Dickson et al. (ibid.) further question the cultural limitations of leadership knowledge gleaned from literature. Barakat and Brooks (2016) question leaders' responses to the dynamics of globalization in education in practice, thus exploring globalization as one of the consequences leading to cultural conflict. Notwithstanding the glorification of its benefits within the world community, globalization has also been criticized due to the possibility of cultural and intellectual colonization, as well as the danger of educational commodification (Darling-Hammond & Lieberman, 2012). How does this play out within the various education contexts in the 'fractured' Mediterranean milieu?

Alvesson and Sveningsson (2003) demolish the model of the heroic leader. This issue, therefore, seeks to present an exploration of educational leaders' mundane practices, and perceptions, that enable a textured reading of educational leadership with various layers, rather than conceptualizing leadership as a range of competences and models that are common in many of the popular leadership discourses. This creates a space for the various writers to map the diverse ways in which leadership discourses are received, translated and enacted at practitioner level within the constraints of local and global policy within the Mediterranean region. Alvesson and Spicer (2011) maintain that 'leadership is seldom a matter of a great leader with a clear self-understanding who directs, supports, and controls followers', instead it is best understood as 'full of ambiguities, paradoxes, confusions, inconsistencies' (p. 48).

The Mediterranean Basin is regarded as the cradle of cultures, sciences and knowledge, thus embracing a multicultural tradition while upholding a common culture based on the respect and recognition of diversity, recognizing individuality while being open to embracing 'otherness'. Globalization is bringing about fundamental reform, thus leading to the displacement of reference points and established frameworks. It is the Mediterranean attempting to be a coherent whole, notwithstanding the fractures which divide it and conflicts that are tearing it apart, undoubtedly mirrored at various leadership levels in education institutions.

According to Alvesson and Spicer (2011), 'Leadership easily becomes everything and nothing. And the use of the term easily oscillates between what everybody does and what only an exceptional group of real leaders do' (p. 9). Those exploring leadership are thus encouraged to consider its variation, incoherence and complexity across a multitude of contexts. Shah (2006) draws attention to the knowledge gap in mainstream literature regarding diverse perspectives of educational leadership, thus confirming that ethnocentric concepts, theories and practices in education, predominantly embedded in western philosophy and values, tend to ignore the growing multicultural nature of educational institutions. In other words, 'There is no denying the tensions across conflicting ideological positions and concepts, but this does not negate working towards increased understanding' (p. 377), thus working towards the development of complex theoretical constructs for the reconceptualization of educational leadership. Hammad and Hallinger (2017) question the importance of inquiring into the nature of national, regional, and cultural subsets of the knowledge base in educational leadership and management, asserting that scholarship in this area 'is undergoing a sea change that has elevated the urgency, legitimacy and value of understanding the diversity of school leadership and management practices across the world' (p. 447). Consequently, recent reviews of educational leadership and management research confirm a dramatic rise in the volume of such research in developing countries in the past decade (Hallinger, 2017; Oplatka & Arar, 2017). This thus suggests a movement of scholars studying the diversity of educational leadership and management practices beyond the traditional Anglo-American centers of scholarship in order to examine both the contextualized application of 'Western models' in developing countries, as well as the generation of 'indigenous models' of leadership and management (Akkary, 2014).

The shift to this diversity suggests the unfolding of a cultural turn in educational leadership studies (Wilkinson & Bristol, 2018) that is a basic premise as well of this volume. There is an increasing body of literature and research that is challenging the applicability of the dominant approaches in educational leadership scholarship and practice. This turn is a critical outlook that originates from Post-colonial, Black, Indigenous, and Feminist reflexivity. It relates to the demands for justice coming from the Indigenous in Australia, America, and New Zealand. It connects with the experience of women leading in developing countries, and with the confrontation of values occurring in the unproblematic importation of the Western model of leadership in Asia, the Middle East, and African educational systems.

The cultural turn in educational leadership research reveals how the current research on leadership subjugates knowledge, that is, there is a persistent silence on knowledge about leading and managing that is not compatible with the Western anthropocentric conceptualization of power (suffice to think on the diverse conceptualization of power in Indigenous cultures). Moreover, it draws attention to the increasing heterogeneity of the contemporary composition of the school settings, and thus translating in a call for being culturally responsive. Still, it directs attention to the experiences of women leading in developing countries that are facing complex dilemmas as they struggle between their aspirations and the religious and cultural expectations of the contexts in which they work. It underlines the importance of religion, and the need to look at the intersection of social categories (ethnicity, gender, socioeconomic background) in shaping the conceptualization of educational leadership. It finally leads to understanding the intermeshing of the global, dominant, universal truths of the educational leadership models with the situated and culturally constructed practice of educational leadership. It helps to enrich our understanding of the translation of the global discourses of leadership into local settings and the emergence of cross-cultural values systems that problematize the universalistic assumptions of the Anglo-Saxon models of educational leadership.

The cultural turn invites, therefore, to study educational leadership as a culturally constructed practice. To consider, in other words, its situatedness in a cultural milieu and historical institutional legacy. The use of the category 'culture' deserves some clarifications. To simplify a broad anthropological literature, 'culture' usually outlines the 'glue' of a group of people: those shared and common understandings that distinguish a group of people from other groups. Instead of overemphasizing the unitary character of a culture that conveys a sense of stability and essence, the cultural turn suggests considering 'culture' an open and contested texture. Culture is seen as a process. By taking a distance from an idea of culture as a focus on 'identity' and 'structure', the cultural turn is more interested in underlining the fluidity of 'culture'. It brings to the forefront the making and re-making of culture, the always negotiated character of what constitutes 'culture'. In that sense, the cultural construction of educational leadership is analyzed by looking at how it emerges from the concatenation of global and local configurations of discourses and practices, and at how they are enacted in practice. The cultural turn shifts attention then to the issue of the 'context' of the agency. By reprising a long and still critical discussion on 'context', it reminds us that educational leadership is not without a context, it instead emerges in, and with a context, i.e. it is a situated activity that relates to more extensive societal structures or comes out with the performance of activity (Lave, 1996). It shapes and is shaped by the field of practice in which educational leadership is enacted.

The emphasis on the cultural situatedness of educational leadership is particularly important in the case of the countries of the Mediterranean basin, albeit it has not been sufficiently investigated. The Mediterranean region is usually described as a place of cultural diversity, as a world that is impossible to unify, that is made of people and states that intersect and continually transform, a space of movement to tell with Braudel. It is a place of many histories: a point of meeting, but also the separation between Europe, Africa and Asia. These complexities are not reducible into the dominant perimeters of the discourses of the global reform education movement. There is something that is not translatable in those coordinates: the need to analyze the 'missing-what' of educational leadership in the Mediterranean region.

Intending to start the exploration of what is left out and put aside by the mainstream literature on educational leadership in the Mediterranean region, this volume collects seven reflexive chapters. We asked authors to analyze the dynamics of educational leadership in their countries and critically theorize it. The idea was to mobilize critical repertoires or analyze critically existing theories. The objective was to problematize the philosophies of government, and the underlying assumptions to get a more situated understanding of the enactment of educational leadership. Chapters describe enactments and conceptualizations of educational leadership in EU (Malta, Cyprus, Spain, Portugal and Italy) and non-EU countries (Israel and Algeria) that are located geographically at the intersection of Europe, North Africa and Middle East.

The book opens with a focus on two small EU countries, Malta and Cyprus: two islands of the Mediterranean with a colonial legacy. Denise Mifsud analyzes the educational leadership for social justice discourse and its enactment in Malta. She underlines the paradoxes and the contradictions of this discourse. While generically it is hard to be against 'justice', in practice, 'inclusion' and 'integration' are often ill-defined, or framed within the dominant accountability discourses that make it operational, by considering in the scenario of the comparative exercises of assessment, like PISA, TIMMS, etc. with all the associated risks of translation of 'justice' in very narrow conceptualizations of growth, improvement and managerialism. Mifsud offers a glimpse of the system of education in Malta, of its legacy and the current developments: the attempt to move towards a more decentralized system. She describes an inequitable system of education and the unfolding of educational reforms that aligned with EU discourses of quality and equity in education have little influence in reshaping the reproduction of inequalities. Her research on how educational leaders in Malta enact the current policies reveals the distance between policy and practice. Beyond the idea of equity as only a matter of reducing the achievement gap between low and high achievers, leadership for social justice seems to entail: (a) a student-centered approach, and in particular, a sensibility to cultural differences in an educational setting that is becoming increasingly multicultural and (b) a set of organizational conditions to make equitable school environments a reality. In their chapter on the education system in Cyprus, Petros Pashiardis and Antonios Kafa reflect empirically and theoretically on successful school leadership. They rely on a ten-year research project on educational leadership in primary and secondary schools in order to describe the need for educational leaders to balance between a mix of internal and external dimensions. They describe a highly centralized education system where there is a distance between the configuration of school governance at the macro level and the settings of the local communities and school organizations. Even now, there is little intention to move towards decentralization and school leaders are asked to comply with the governing rules of the system.

Nonetheless, the investigation reveals how school leaders are essential to promote school improvement. Pashiardis and Kafa focus attention, then, on the enactment of successful school leadership in Cyprus. The pillars of the new configuration are: (1) networked leadership developing external relations, (2) people-centered leadership and (3) clear vision and values that give rise to highly contextual combinations. Here, school leaders working in a centralized system are required to develop felicitous assemblages 'among professional and personal attributes that include the participation of internal and external school stakeholders'. Pashiardis and Kafa's chapter illustrates how attention to 'context' is increasingly important even in the literature on school improvement and effectiveness, especially when there is a need to fill the gap between abstract principles and situated practice.

Three chapters of the book pay attention, instead, to the dynamics of educational leadership in Spain, Portugal and Italy. Usually, these three countries are grouped with Greece in the category of the South Europe Welfare State model. They are also peripheral countries in the sense of the world system theory, named often in derogatory terms with the acronym 'PIGS'. In these countries, the knowledge policy is dominated by the rhetoric of New Public Management. Educational leadership figures prominently as a critical policy to promote the agenda of school improvement: managerialistic approaches and vocabularies are recurrent inspirations that marginalize alternative conceptualizations.

In his chapter on Spain, Enrique Javier Díez Gutiérrez describes the shift from the democratic form of school governance to a top-down hierarchical model. The implementation of a new regulation (the LOMCE Act) meant the significant reduction of the democratic participation in the life of the school and the increasing diminishing educational role of school leaders that are asked to orient their agency to effectiveness, instead of pedagogical considerations. The new structure of governance tends to realize the McDonaldization of schools. School leaders are transformed in managers responsible for finance, business and human resources. Schools are enacted as 'pyramidal hierarchies' with adverse effects in terms of motivation and development of mutual relationships of trust and cooperation. Paradoxically, this process is accompanied by a rhetoric of decentralization and autonomy. Apparently, schools are given more liberty to decide; in practice, a process of curriculum centralization is taking place, and increasing control is established on educational actions. A logic of school competitions for resources is therefore set as a form of government that risks enhancing instead to reduce the existing inequalities in a situation where severe public spending cuts are decided.

Similarly, in their chapter on Portugal, Maria Assunção Flores and Fernando Ilídio Ferreira underline how the introduction of the discourse of leadership in 2008 implied the demise of the democratic participation to school-decision making. While formerly school leaders were elected, in the new legislation they were appointed by the state. Further, a discourse drawing on efficiency, effectiveness, quality management and leadership replaced the democratic discourse. By considering the importance of the context for the exercise of educational leadership, Maria Assunção Flores and Fernando Ilídio Ferreira's investigation on headteachers reveals, however: (a) the persistence of the idea of 'democratic leadership', even if the model of the school governance has been completely restructured, (b) the need for school leaders to find a balance between contradictory demands, given by the intersection and sometimes conflicting overlaps between the managerialistic, education and community logics that characterize the organizational field of education policy.

In the same vein, a 'war of discourses' between bureaucracy, managerial, professional and democratic principles outlines the coordinates of school leaders' agency in Italy, as suggested by Danilo Taglietti and Paolo Landri. This war feeds unsolved contradictions and dilemmas in the everyday life of headteachers: still involved in the legacy of the past configurations of the educational governance, they are not entirely aligned, regardless of the rhetorics, to a managerial practice that is business oriented. This complexity is enhanced by the digital governance of education that is introducing platforms, software and data. Here, school leadership unfolds as a paper-digital-human assemblage and envisages a multiplication of the presence of school leaders. Accordingly, the study of educational leadership seems to require a more fine-detailed of its dynamics that rethinks the dominant humanistic approach to school organization.

Contradictions and complexities also emerge in analyzing conceptualizations and enactments of educational leadership in Algeria and Israel. In her chapter, Devorah Kalekin-Fishman focuses on three regimes of practice in Israel: (a) the Ministry of Education, (b) a private school where Hebrew is the language of instruction and (c) a public school in which Arabic is the language of instruction. The chapter illustrates the complex scenario of the education system in Israel that includes many subdivisions related to religion, language, community and curriculum differentiation while preserving its integrity as a system through a strategy of centralization. She concludes that educational leadership is not about implementing heroic and marvellous plans. Instead, it rather implies enacting a practice that develops in a logic of complex adaptive systems. This logic suggests considering the complexity of histories, and traditions of each educational setting and confronting the situation at hand by understanding the constraints, the freedom and the potential for alternative agency. In the final chapter on Algeria, Milani draws attention to the educational reform in that country, and notably at the university. Here, the influence of the EU mirrors in a reform inspired by the Bologna process. The goal of the reform was to improve the state of the university, by the alignment to a discourse of modernization that stresses the link between university and economy. Unfortunately, this reform was carried out in a top-down fashion with little involvement of university leaders. The case highlights the failure of an educational reform when there is scarce consideration of its context of implementation. In this situation, leaders swing between compliance, compromise and routine.

Overall, these chapters illustrate how the dominant discourses and policies of educational leadership in seven countries of the Mediterranean basin are aligned with the universalistic assumptions of the epistemology of the school improvement and efficiency model. These discourses have substituted earlier models of governance (like in Spain, Portugal and Italy), leading to the enactment of a hierarchical model of school organization and reinforcement of centralistic configuration. In practice, educational leadership in these countries implies a capacity to balance competing and sometimes challenging demands while the organizational fields are becoming more and more complicated due to the presence of a different logic of governance (performativity, managerialism, democracy) and the multiplication of heterogeneity of the social and cultural environments. Additional investigations and explorations in other countries of the Mediterranean are needed. Nevertheless, a promising line of enquiry is outlined for giving more space to the actual conditions of the cultural construction of educational leadership while problematizing the universalistic principles of the dominant discourses.

References

Akkary, R. K. (2014). The role and role context of the Lebanese school principal: Toward a culturally grounded understanding of the principalship. *Educational Management Administration and Leadership*, 42(5), 718–742.

Alvesson, M., & Spicer, A. (Eds.). (2011). *Metaphors we lead by: Understanding leadership in the real world*. Routledge.

Alvesson, M., & Spicer, A. (2012). Critical leadership studies: The case for critical performativity. *Human Relations, 65*(3), 367–390.

Alvesson, M., & Sveningsson, S. (2003). Managers doing leadership: The extra-ordinarization of the mundane. *Human Relations, 56*(12), 1435–1459.

Barakat, M., & Brooks, J. S. (2016). When globalization causes cultural conflict: Leadership in the context of an Egyptian/American school. *Journal of Cases in Educational Leadership, 19*(4), 3–15.

Christie, P., & Lingard, L. (2001, April 10–14). *Capturing complexity in educational leadership.* Paper presented at the American Educational Research Association Conference, Seattle.

Darling-Hammond, L., & Lieberman, A. (2012). *Teacher quality and school development: Teacher education around the world: Changing policies and practices.* Routledge.

Dickson, M. W., Castano, N., Magomaeva, A., & Den Hartog, D. N. (2012). Conceptualizing leadership across cultures. *Journal of World Business, 47*, 483–492.

Fairhurst, G. T. (2011). *The power of framing: Creating the language of leadership.* Jossey-Bass.

Festinger, L. (1957). *A theory of cognitive dissonance.* Row Peterson.

Hallinger, P. (2017). Revealing a hidden literature: Systematic research on educational leadership and management in Africa. *Educational Management Administration and Leadership, 51*(5), 618–637.

Hammad, W., & Hallinger, P. (2017). A systematic review of conceptual models and methods used in research on educational leadership and management in Arab societies. *School Leadership & Management: Formerly School Organisation, 37*(5), 434–456.

Ladkin, D. (2010). *Rethinking leadership: A new look at old leadership questions.* Edward Elgar Publishing Limited.

Lave, J. (1996). The practice of learning. In C. Seth & J. Lave (Eds.), *Understanding practice. Perspective on activity and context* (pp. 3–34). Cambridge University Press.

Niesche, R. (2011). *Foucault and educational leadership: Disciplining the principal.* Routledge.

Oplatka, I., & Arar, K. (2017). The research on educational leadership and management in the Arab world since the 1990s: A systematic review. *Review of Education, 5*(3), 267–307.

Shah, S. (2006). Educational leadership: An Islamic perspective. *British Educational Research Journal, 32*(3), 363–385.

Wilkinson, J., & Bristol, L. (Eds.). (2018). *Educational leadership as a culturally-constructed practice: New directions and possibilities.* Routledge.

Wood, M., & Case, P. (2006). Editorial: Leadership refrains – Again, again and again. *Leadership, 292,* 139–145.

CHAPTER 2

Social Justice and Education in the Maltese State School System: Some Political and Practical Issues

Denise Mifsud

Abstract

Educators have had good reason to be concerned with social justice in a context where diversity has become more pronounced in both our schools and communities, with widening divisions between the advantaged and the disadvantaged (Ryan, 2006). Internationally, increasing emphasis has been placed on utilizing the role of school leadership to address issues of social justice and equality (Bogotch, 2008). This is unfolding within a scenario where comparative studies of the performance of educational systems, such as PISA, TIMSS and PIRLS, dominate the policy imagination globally, which assessment regimes have led to increased pressure on school systems. Locally, the issues of social justice and equity in education are being addressed via curricular and policy-oriented reform, within a society welcoming an ever-increasing influx of migrants and a local economic reality with identified skills shortages. It is within such a local Euro-Mediterranean context that this chapter seeks to explore how issues of social justice and equity are addressed at both policy and practitioner level. In-depth, semi-structured interviews with the Heads of both a Primary and a Secondary State School with an ethnically-diverse student population provide a narrative of leadership for social justice, while allowing for a critique of how policies are being perceived and enacted in practice. Leadership and social justice not being natural bedfellows (Ryan, 2006), with social justice being culturally constructed (Arar & Oplatka, 2016), these headmasters' narratives provide an understanding as to how personal, cultural and national contexts contribute to the enactment of social justice leadership. What criteria can we use to judge whether an educational policy or practice is socially just? How do we make comparative assessments of social justice in education? The findings of this small-scale study have implications for other national systems within the Euro-Mediterranean region, particularly those who are concerned with addressing issues of social justice and equity via schooling.

Keywords

equity – inclusion – leadership – multiculturalism – performance – policy discourses – social justice

1   Introduction

This chapter seeks to explore how issues of social justice and equity are addressed at both policy and practitioner level within a local Euro-Mediterranean education context. Francis et al. (2017) highlight that the advancement of social justice in state education is complicated and contested in multiple ways both due to the distinct definitions of social justice, in addition to the fact that its meaning in practice is not straightforward either in terms of educational purposes and content, nor in terms of modes of organization and delivery. Notwithstanding,

> If the school system is dealing unjustly with some of its pupils, they are not the only ones to suffer. The quality of education for all the others is degraded … The issue of social justice is not an add-on. It is fundamental to what good education is about. (Connell, 1993, p. 15)

Locally, the issues of social justice and equity in education are being addressed via curricular and policy-oriented reform. Malta's acquisition of independence from British rule in 1964 has triggered a number of revolutionary reforms that the Maltese education sector has been experiencing ever since, all underlined by widening access of education provision to all. More recently, the focus on equity and social justice has been earmarked by the publication of the following policy documents: *National Curriculum Framework* (2012), *Learning Outcomes Framework* (2015), *Framework for the Education Strategy for Malta 2014–2024* (2014) and *My Journey* (2016). This policyscape is unfolding within a society welcoming an ever-increasing influx of migrants and a local economic reality with identified skills shortages. This chapter presents a problematization of the social justice concept within education as presented in the literature, while setting out to critique this concept as an educational goal, as well as the role educational leadership is expected to play in the promotion of equity and social justice discourses. This is followed by a detailed overview of the local policy landscape. The voices of two local school leaders project readings of the various factors that impinge on the unfolding of social justice in the Maltese education system. While I recognize that Malta is not necessarily indicative of global issues and policy trends, I suggest that the themes that emerge are valid beyond this context, mainly due to the increasing globalization of education policy (Ball 2013) and the global extension of practices of policy borrowing widely established among Western nations (Lingard, 2010; Whitty et al., 2016) that may have resonance within the Euro-Mediterranean region.

2 What Is Social Justice? Problematizing the Elusive Concept within the Schooling Context

At the dawn of the twenty-first century, which is now moving beyond two decades, the term 'social justice' is appearing in numerous public texts and discourses within the education field, thus becoming a key concept in current education policy and practice (Clark, 2006; North, 2006). Moreover, the concept of social justice is crucial to theorizing about education and schooling, consequently being considered by politicians, policymakers and practitioners in their thinking about the nature of education and the purpose of schools. Regrettably, education practitioners, researchers and policymakers often utilize this umbrella term (social justice) while leaving out salient details about its social, cultural, economic, and political bearing. Notwithstanding the unanimous agreement on the desirability of social justice as an educational goal, this is complemented by a parallel contestation over its actual meaning and application in relation to schooling, that is, in relation to the formulation of policy and how it is to be included in practice.

According to Cambron-McCabe and McCarthy (2005), 'The prevalence of social justice language in educational settings and scholarship portends a new movement with as many meanings as actors on the scene. This visibility is cause for celebration as well as unease' (p. 202). Despite the centrality of social justice issues in education, not enough prominence has been attributed to the precise meaning of social justice discourse (Gewirtz, 2002), with social justice being regarded as 'an *old* but not an *old-fashioned* concept' (Arar et al., 2017, p. 192, original emphasis). Literature refers to the elusive meaning of social justice and the lack of clarity of the term. The 'conceptual plurality' (Liasidou & Antoniou, 2015, p. 348) of this ambiguous and contested notion derives from one's 'epistemological commitments and theoretical preferences' (Johnson, 2008, p. 310).

Ryan (2006) attempts to explore the difficulties behind the definition of the concept. This is due to the multitude of versions that exist, coupled with inherent ambiguities and contradictions within these definitions. Moreover, many of the approaches are simply unreasonable and unfeasible. Most social justice commentators concede that it revolves around legitimacy, fairness, welfare and inclusion. Clark (2006) outlines the philosophical constituents of the social justice concept as the 'perfect world argument', 'just society', 'educated citizens', 'just schools' and 'school instrumentality' in enabling these social justice interests. In a perfect world, social justice is not a relevant consideration – it can only be invoked as a ground for policy and practice if the difference leads to an inequality which offends against a principle deemed to be constitutive of a fair society. At the heart of a just society lies equality as a regulatory principle. It is debatable which form this equality ought to take: equality of opportunity, equality of treatment, equality of outcome. Citizens are not naturally endowed with a spirit of social justice, hence its importance as an aim of education. Schools must subsequently be so arranged as to achieve this end. Consequently, the school as a social institution may be regarded as an instrument to be used in the interests of social justice, with instrumentality being both internal and external.

Ryan (2006) explores the use of inclusion/exclusion as a lens for addressing social justice issues. Students can be excluded from school premises, learning processes and activities because of ability, age, race, class, gender, sexuality and poverty. This approach shifts the blame away from individuals, thus uncovering the taken-for-granted role of institutions and systems in shaping the unequal human relations, and the unjust distribution of goods, rights and responsibilities. Barad (2007) argues convincingly that justice

> is not a state that can be achieved once and for all. There are no solutions. There is only the ongoing practice of being open and alive, each intra-action, so that we might use our ability to respond, our responsibility, to help awaken, to breathe life into ever new possibilities for living justly. (p. x)

Thus, the presence of tensions within social justice categories. North (2006) depicts the three social justice categories of redistribution/recognition, sameness/difference and macro/micro level forces as multidirectional, intersecting spheres, in that these seemingly dichotomous categories often overlap and remain in tension with each other, with the possibility of friction and contradiction within and among spheres. These complex, fraught interactions that emerge when various conceptualizations of social justice collide aid in the promotion of continued dialogue and reflexivity on the aims and potential of education for social justice.

3   Social Justice as an Educational Goal

Educators have had good reason to be concerned with social justice in a context where diversity has become more pronounced in both our schools and communities, with widening divisions between the advantaged and the disadvantaged (Ryan, 2006). Consequently, it comes as no surprise that educators, policymakers, as well as the general public are increasingly conscious of the fact that in spite of the numerous well-intentioned restructuring, reform, and curricular efforts, many children who are in some way diverse from the previously dominant and traditionally most successful White, middle class children are not achieving school success, with 'success' being translated in terms of access to a wide range of teaching, learning and achievements related to the development of an 'educated citizen' (Shields, 2004).

Mowat (2018) states that 'the quest to address inequities in educational outcomes associated with socio-economic status is not new, is enduring and is of global significance' (p. 300). She puts forward the case that the problem cannot be tackled via a primary and exclusive focus on the school as the agent of change, but on addressing endemic inequalities within society. Income inequalities have been growing steadily within most OECD countries, being at their peak within the last three decades (OECD, 2016). Social class is closely associated with student and school characteristics, thereby wielding a powerful influence on learning outcomes and student achievement (Schleicher, 2014). OECD highlights the salient attributes of top-performing education systems as having high expectations of all pupils with a specific prominence on equity. This data is derived from the Programme for International Student Assessment (PISA), within a culture of performativity in which nation states are fuelled by international league tables (Ball, 2003, 2015). Harris et al. (2015) question the viability of such comparative international reports that seem to suggest that the replication of strategies in new contexts will automatically result in better outcomes. The complexity of school systems together with the contextual and cultural boundaries in which they function are thus disregarded. How is equity being perceived in OECD reports (Boyum, 2014)? Furthermore, Schleicher (2014) critiques the OECD who frame the problem in terms of what education systems, schools and teachers can do in order to redress inequalities in society, rather than how redressing inequalities in society can lead to more equitable educational outcomes. This leads to a 'blame culture' in which the entire school community is held accountable and responsible for the circumstances in which it finds itself and for solutions to the problem (Smyth & Wrigley, 2015). Notwithstanding, the OECD does seem to be veering in the other direction of relating educational equity to equity more broadly in society, 'Education's powerful role does not mean that it can work alone. Reducing inequality also requires policies for housing, criminal justice, taxation and health care to work hand in hand with education to make a lasting difference' (OECD, 2016, p. 10).

Comparative studies of the performance of educational systems govern the global policyscape, thus leading to increased pressure on school systems.

One particular example is the PISA assessment regime (OECD, 2014) that steers schools to focus solely on an improvement agenda in order to reduce the achievement gap between the groups of high-attaining and low-attaining learners, especially targeting those groups who continue to be marginalized in school education. Thus, within the context of globalization, nations increasingly turn to policy borrowing as a solution to identified problems, with the current policy focus being actively concerned with closing the attainment gap. However, the relationship between policy generation and enactment is not linear, with various points of translation, and mistranslation, of policy intentions (Reeves & Drew, 2012). Forde and Torrance (2017) consequently deem that,

> There is a danger that unidimensional and politically expedient solutions will be generated that are short term and largely concerned with targeting individual pupils to improve their examination scores rather than looking at systemic change to address the needs of diverse learners. (p. 117)

Gewirtz (2006) thus argues that social justice in education is both level and context dependent, outlining that cross-national or other comparative assessments of social justice cannot be made without taking into account the various modes in which justice is enacted in practice. Indeed,

> What criteria can we use to judge whether an educational policy or practice is socially just? How do we make comparative assessments of social justice in education? In other words, how can we tell whether one national or local education system or one educational institution or one educational policy or practice is more socially just than another? (p. 70)

The significance of justice can only be properly comprehended within particular settings of interpretation and enactment.

Shields (2004) argues that

> difference is normal. It is neither to be celebrated nor denigrated. The differences in our schools provide a rich tapestry of human existence that must be the starting point for a deeply democratic, academically excellent, and socially just education. No one is defined by a single factor or characteristic ... Difference is an inescapable and foundational quality of our society and our education system. (pp. 127–128)

4 Educational Leadership in Relation to Discourses of Equity and Social Justice

Internationally, increasing emphasis has been placed on utilizing the role of school leadership to address issues of social justice and equality in terms of educational policy, theory and professional practice (Bogotch, 2008; Blackmore, 2009). This is unfolding within a scenario where comparative studies of the performance of educational systems, such as PISA, TIMMS and PIRLS, dominate the policy imagination globally, which assessment regimes have led to increased pressure on school systems. An emergent significant factor is the achievement gap between groups of high-attaining and low-attaining learners (Forde & Torrance, 2017). Consequently, there has been particular concern with how issues of social justice and equity are shaped by broader neoliberal rationalities, regimes and practices, including new managerialism, high-stakes testing and accountabilities. These have been enacted within discourses of growth, marketization, competition, choice, improvement, standardization, meritocracy, performativity, managerialism and school autonomy. Accordingly, these powerful global reforms have reshaped social justice priorities in schools to a very narrow focus on the 'private' goals of education (social efficiency and social mobility) at the expense of 'public' goals (democratic and citizenship goals) (Niesche & Keddie, 2016).

Literature thus contends that 'educational leadership and social justice are, and must be, inextricably interconnected' (Bogotch & Shields, 2014, p. 10). Middlewood (2007) further explains that for educators, leadership for social justice comprises the confrontation of 'major issues, such as those of equity, diversity and inclusion, in stimulating the changes needed for the embedding of social justice' (p. vii). It is also acknowledged that the concepts of leadership and social justice are discursive constructs present in specific economic, political and social realities, as such being highly contested notions (Niesche & Keddie, 2016). Oplatka and Arar (2016) in turn problematize the notion of leadership for social justice as constructed in dominant Western ideologies, reaching the simple conclusion that 'traditional societies need a particular conceptualization of leadership for social justice that is based on entrenched social norms giving unique meanings to issues of justice, respect, interpersonal relations, equality and equity in education' (p. 366). Any attempt to impose Western-based concepts of social justice and leadership on the educational systems of diverse societies is a foregone conclusion. Despite international interest in social justice leadership, there is the need to explore its meaning in different contexts (Bryant et al., 2014), as well as the contested nature of leadership itself and its relationship with the discourses of social justice and equity (Niesche & Keddie, 2016). Ryan (2006) sums this up very aptly when he implies that,

> Leadership and social justice are not natural bedfellows; nor are leadership and inclusion. The extent to which leadership meshes with social justice or inclusion depends on the way in which leadership is conceived, that is, in the way that relationships are envisioned among members of institutions, in the roles that are prescribed for individuals and groups, and in the ends to which leadership activities are directed. (p. 7)

Oplatka and Arar (2016) identify four major elements of leadership for social justice that have been analyzed in the educational leadership literature, exercising scepticism and critique in terms of their compatibility with the value system of traditional society. These elements comprise a decrease in achievement gaps; the intensification of social justice in schools; the incorporation of democratic/ethical values; as well as the fostering of critical dialogues and consciousness. An inherent paradox can also be detected between the social justice leadership model theorized in the West, and the major features of traditional society. These contradictions are present in the dichotomies of individual versus collective orientation; ascription versus achievement; particularistic versus universalistic relationships; autocracy versus democracy; and maintenance versus innovativeness. This eventually leads readers to pose the following question: 'What does it mean to practise socially just educational leadership?' Departing from the position that considers inclusion as the main value of socially just educational leadership, Capper and Young (2014) identify five incongruities and constraints that co-exist within the exercise of such leadership. The authors question the actual meaning of inclusive practice, as well as the interchangeable use of the terms 'inclusion' and 'integration', stating that the concept of inclusion remains 'marginalized, ill-defined, and undebated' (ibid., p. 159) within the educational leadership for social justice discourse. One finds a paucity of literature that examines the intersection of identity and difference due to its focus on separate student identity groups. The field of educational leadership for social justice is divided on the emphasis given to the issue of academic achievement, to the detriment of other benefits of schooling. Moreover, evidence exists of the lack of policy and practice coherence to address inequities. Furthermore, the practice of social justice leadership should be the norm, rather than the exception, calling for the combination rather than separation of super-heroes from critical collaborative leadership.

School-led social justice practice drives leaders into 'perilous politics' (Whang, 2019, p. 118) due to its commitment to the critique of social prejudice, thus leading to political risks in the potential evocation of a breakdown in social relationships. School leaders are advised to develop 'a new and more open approach to difference ... [to] ensure that educators do not celebrate some legitimate differences and pathologize others' (Shields, 2004, p. 128).

5 Setting the Scene: The Local Policy Landscape

Malta benefited from British rule for almost two centuries – it gained independence in 1964, became a Republic in 1974 and consequently joined the European Union in 2004 – it therefore goes without saying that national education provision in our islands closely follows the British model (Sultana, 1997). The political change that took place in 1964, when Malta acquired independence from British rule, triggered a number of revolutionary reforms that the Maltese education sector has been experiencing ever since. The main educational milestones since independence are the provision of secondary education for all in 1970; increasing the school leaving age from 14 to 16 in 1974; the 1988 Education Act that established the provision of state compulsory education for all Maltese citizens; the recognition of the professional status of teachers, the setting up of School Councils, and the creation of the first National Minimum Curriculum in 1989, among other initiatives. Notwithstanding, these last two decades have been extremely significant for the Maltese educational scenario due to several major measures and restructurings that have been implemented. These underline attempts to augment the country's intellectual capital and provide improved quality education with the aim of enabling all Maltese children to succeed. The common thread running through these reforms is the widening of access to education, thus being in line with the politics of social justice.

The Maltese educational system has been undergoing a structured, gradual but steady change in terms of decentralization and increased school autonomy, with the main aim being that of renewal – modernizing it in line with global policy development. This modernization was initiated by the publication of *Tomorrow's schools: Developing effective learning cultures* (Wain et al., 1995) – this document indicated a starting point for an examination of current policies and practices considering the demands made by a fast-changing world. This document paved the way for a revised *National Minimum Curriculum* (NMC) published in 1999, establishing compulsory schooling as the start of a lifelong process of education. This initiation of the decentralization process in the Maltese educational system was meant to provide schools with more flexibility and power in order to be in a better position to cater for the needs of their students through an enhanced teaching and learning process. All these changes paved the way for the basic principles underpinning *For all children to succeed* (Ministry of Education, Youth and Employment, 2005) – the policy document that brought about the introduction of state school networks according to their geographical location.

This structural reform led to further reform aspects, being closely followed by an amendment to the Education Act (House of Representatives, 2006) and the agreement between the Government of Malta and the Malta Union of Teachers (July 2007), paving the way for the setting up of ten colleges. Furthermore, as a result of the schools college reform, in November 2008, the Ministry of Education published a policy document about the transition of students from primary to secondary schools under the college system, *Transition from primary to secondary schools in Malta* (Ministry of Education, Youth and Employment, 2008). This proposed mixed-ability classes throughout the primary school years, eliminating the hitherto streamed primary classes in the final two years, followed by the phasing out of the 11+ examination – thus enabling a smoother flow from one level of education to another.

An agreement on the synchronization of church compulsory schooling with state provision in 2009 led to the abolition of the 11+ examination two years later, thus providing a more level playing field and increasing student heterogeneity in all schools. Consequently, the new end-of-primary benchmark was launched. A review of the NMC, initiated in 2009 led to the *National Curriculum Framework* (NCF) that was translated into law in 2012 – a framework that replaced discriminatory educational arrangements with comprehensive ones in a bid to promote progress for all learners. This is the first curriculum framework to be adopted since Malta joined the EU in 2004, with its proposal for universal education entitlement espousing six general principles, and built around eight learning areas, inspired by the EU eight Key Competences Framework. This NCF addresses the gaps in our learning processes that over the years have led to absenteeism, to significant rates of early school leavers and to low skills and competences for a proportion of students. It is intended to lead to an increased participation rate in post-secondary and tertiary education and attract more students to lifelong learning, encouraging them to embark on further and higher education streams. One of the aims of the NCF is the introduction of additional equity and decentralization in the national system, particularly through its proposed *Learning Outcomes Framework* (LOF). This LOF, with its gradual implementation commencing in the scholastic year 2018/2019 is intended to lead to more curricular autonomy of colleges and schools by addressing individual learning needs through the freedom from centrally-imposed knowledge-centric syllabi.

Another recent landmark in compulsory education has been the launch of a *Framework for the Education Strategy for Malta 2014–2024*, based on the four values of equity, social justice, inclusivity and diversity, in order to provide generations with skills and talents for employability and citizenship in the twenty-first century, thus aiming to reduce the gaps in education outcomes, reduce the high incidence of early school-leavers, and increase participation in lifelong learning. The Framework for the Education Strategy for Malta (2014–2024) document confirms that the Education Ministry positions itself at the forefront to provide present and future generations with the necessary skills and talents for employability and citizenship in the 21st century. This framework has been further complimented by the launch of *MyJourney* (Ministry for Education and Employment, 2016), a major reform in the secondary school system to be available from 2019/2020 which will see the educational sector move from a 'one-size-fits-all' system to a more inclusive and equal programme through the choice of academic, vocational or applied subjects that will have equal parity of esteem at MQF (Malta Qualification Framework) Level 3, irrespective of the route taken.

Education for all: Special needs and inclusive education in Malta (European Agency for Special Needs and Inclusive Education, 2014) is a report commissioned by the Minister for Education and Employment that examines special needs education provision in Malta. The main findings reveal an education system that reinforces an integrative approach for some learners, rather than an inclusive one for all; school level practices that do not foster inclusion; in addition to a lack of equity and full participation for all. This audit identified a number of priority steps in order for inclusion to be taken up as a whole-school approach among which are creating clarity around the concept of inclusion; re-focusing support to colleges and schools; establishing a national education training body; supporting all schools in teaching for diversity as well as the use of evidence-based teaching and learning; in addition to promoting self-review at all levels of the system. These suggestions are being implemented gradually across the education system. This led to the drafting and eventual launch of *A Policy on Inclusive Education in Schools* and *A National Inclusive Education Framework* (Ministry for Education and Employment, 2019a, 2019b), that embrace the concept, values and principles of inclusive education into the realm of responding positively to all learners' diversity. These aim to bring together all the stakeholders in order to create a school environment conducive to learning, thereby giving all learners the education they are entitled to.

In the meantime, other realities have been unfolding gradually alongside the major reforms happening in the education policyscape. One such recent reform is the introduction of co-education. Although this has been common practice across the state, church and independent sectors at primary level and in the latter sector at secondary level, it was introduced in state secondary schools in 2013 as an ongoing pilot project. Mid-year examinations in state schools were replaced by continuous formative assessment. Other novelties that were introduced in order to bring about the projected provision of an equitable quality education are the introduction of vocational education and training (VET) subjects at secondary level (which are set to increase considerably through *MyJourney*) and a specific focus on e-learning, among others. Due to unprecedented developments within the country's economy thus leading to a new social and cultural reality, teachers have to operate within a globalised environment with an ever-increasing influx of migrants and a local economic reality with identified skills shortages. To partly address this situation and thus improve the integration of migrant children, a Third Country National Co-Ordinator was appointed to advise schools in 2013, with the setting up of the Migrant Learners' Unit later. New challenges, previously non-existent, have been brought about by this situation in terms of language issues, religious beliefs, and the differing expectations of parents.

Overall, Malta occupies a joint 15th place on the EU Social Justice Index. However, when it comes to equitable education, Malta features at the bottom of the EU standings in the area of equitable education (EU Social Index, 2017). Consequently, the European Commission has once again called on Malta to strengthen access to education in its 2019 country-specific recommendations. This therefore points to a very serious achievement gap that is evident in erratic instruction quality, large numbers of under-achievers, school-level variance in achievement, comparatively low participation rates at post-secondary level, gender disparities in achievement, curricular experiences which are not designed to enhance equity in access to education, restricted access to daycare provision and investment in early childhood provision below EU average. Borg (2019) argues that,

> The realities of the Maltese education system challenge the narrative of equal opportunities for all, reflected in the provision of free universal education from kindergarten to university. In fact, such a system structurally and organizationally has served middle-class students much more than their working-class counterparts. For far too long, this education system has appeared meritocratic while being savagely selective beyond meritocracy. (p. 3)

Malta has kept step with EU countries in practically all EU education benchmarks. Additionally, in recent years, Malta has participated for the first time in the TIMSS, PIRLS and PISA international studies. These confirmed that whilst our top achievers compare well with those of other countries, we have an unacceptably high level of low achievers. The EU2020 target is to have less than 15% of the student population classified as 'low achievers'. Borg (2019) further argues that for the past two decades, the official narrative of the educational scene has been defined by a series of official documents based on a discourse promoting diversity, inclusion and entitlement, thus leaning towards a more child-centered and needs-oriented educational system. Notwithstanding,

> the ideological terrain remained largely rooted in the politics of segregation. What was happening at a very fast pace in terms of educational reform was not a revolution from below but a passive revolution, *prescribed* by progressive individuals, who somehow *infiltrated* corridors of power, came close to the zones of decision-making, occupied the right spaces, and from their strategic position managed to influence policy. (p. 5, original emphasis)

6 Methodology

The data for this small-scale study was collected via in-depth, open-ended interviews with two Heads of School which allowed greater flexibility and freedom for both the researcher and the researched. Both Heads, one from the primary sector and the other from the secondary sector, were selected due to the composition of the school population that contains many migrant students hailing from foreign countries. The interviews were recorded and transcribed, followed by the thematic analysis of the empirical data. This small-scale study was conducted in full compliance of research ethics norms. Anonymity and confidentiality are respected as neither participant nor institution names appear or any other means of personal identification. The two participants have been labelled as PH and SH in order to distinguish the school sector (primary and secondary).

The following are the interview questions:
- Recount your professional life story. What factors made you decide to pursue this leadership role?
- What do you understand by 'social justice'?
- What are your views on the fostering of social justice within the current education policy scenario?
- How do you enact leadership for social justice in your school?
- What are the facilitators for social justice in schools?

- What are the hindrances for social justice in schools?
- What changes/improvements do you envisage for future leaders of social justice?
- How did you learn to become a social justice leader?

The next section presents the main themes that emerged from the empirical data analysis.

7 Analysis and Discussion: Education for Social Justice from the Voices of the Leaders

Analysis of the interview data revealed three main thematic trends around which the findings of this small-scale study are presented below. These deal with: (1) Headteachers' perceptions of social justice; (2) their critique of the social justice discourse in the local policy scenario; (3) facilitators and hindrances to the enactment of social justice in schools.

7.1 *Headteachers' Perceptions of Social Justice*

While recounting their professional trajectory, it became evident that both Heads moved from teaching to a senior management position due to their innate desire to promote social justice as an educational goal. This could be brought about through a change in career that saw them move from the classroom to the Headteacher's office. In the words of PH, 'I like change. I think that change is important in life'. SH reiterates that she was very happy as a teacher, 'but at a certain point you decide to go for a change'. Social justice (or the lack of it) has different meanings according to the school environment, thus manifesting itself in diverse ways. This comes out in the narrative of SH who moved to a secondary school after teaching at a post-secondary institution for almost two decades.

> As Assistant Head, I could see that I was making a difference – this role served as an eye-opener towards a completely different class of students that I had never met at Sixth Form: the very poor students, the ones who didn't even have enough to eat, and the ones with social problems … I didn't even know they existed in Gozo … It was a culture shock at first, but then you work with them and see how much difference you can make.

On the other hand, spending most of his headship career within the same school aided PH in the promotion of social justice:

> On my appointment as Head of school, the Director of Human Resources informed me that I just need to move a few metres and change my office! Staying in the same school helped a lot because I knew the teachers, the parents, I had already got used to all the pupils, was familiar with the school culture ... so the shift was quite easy.

Both Heads conceptualized the term social justice in terms of the provision of equality – at the heart of a just society lies equality as a regulatory principle (Clark, 2006). For SH, social justice means

> that every person is given his rights, his freedom to pursue his own dreams. Some people seem to have more accessibility to pursuing certain dreams than others ... For me that is a complete injustice. Social justice would be balancing these things out and not leaving a gap.

Both Heads argue that equality of opportunity and equality of treatment will eventually lead to equality of outcome.

> Social justice is providing ... creating equal opportunities for all to succeed, basically, that everyone has the same opportunity. We all know that within society, not everyone is the same ... The same goes for a school. We have students coming from certain family backgrounds, from deprived backgrounds, so at school, social justice means that despite all these differences, the school has to provide equal opportunities for all the students. Not for the highflyers only, neither for those that are slow learners, but for all the learners. (PH)

The school as a social institution is regarded as an instrument to push forward the interests of social justice, with school instrumentality being both internal and external (Clark, 2006), involving the educators as insiders and the parents as outsiders. These stakeholders are vital to the enactment of social justice as will be discussed further on.

7.2 *Social Justice in the Current Policy Scenario*

The common thread running through education reform in the Maltese policy scenario for the past three decades has been a focus on improved quality education provision with the aim of enabling all Maltese children to succeed. The recognition of the vitality of the widening access to education is in line with the politics of social justice being propagated by the global education policy discourses. SH is of the opinion 'that the education arena is doing a lot to cater for these social injustices starting from the very young, like pre-kinder', with widespread provision being there from the pre-compulsory schooling level of early childhood education. Both Headteachers are aligned with a social justice discourse, in turn problematizing the current role of schooling and its contribution to the intensification of social injustice. PH specifically criticizes the 'modus operandi' of certain teachers who fail to foster social justice:

> It is not easy to foster social justice in schools ... there have been a lot of changes in previous years ... Obviously teachers have to keep up with these changes ... it depends a lot on the teacher's character and mentality as to whether he adjusts to change or not.

He also reiterates how policy intention fails to materialize in reception and actual enactment in the classroom:

> A lot of policies were drawn up in order to foster more social justice ... I fear that the mentality of certain teachers is not in tune with the documents being issued, there are those who have a set mindset and refuse to change ... When it comes to differentiated teaching and learning, it is written in policy documents, but how many teachers have really understood what it means and are actually practising it within the classroom? Are they including all students in the teaching and learning process? ... The teachers themselves have to strive to be protagonists, not just spectators, in the sense that they have to be part of the system and believe in what they are doing ... It's very important for the teachers to own the policies, not just read the policies, make them their own, and then practise them in their everyday life in the classroom, which goes far beyond the mere teaching and learning of academic subjects ... A lot of attempts to foster social justice are being made, but I don't know how far they are being translated into concrete results.

This reflects the findings of Liasidou and Antoniou (2015) whereby educators inadvertently contributed to the maintenance of the status quo that widens the gap between advantaged and disadvantaged students.

PH problematizes the concept of inclusion as it unfolds in class:

> What about inclusion, a topic about which we've heard a lot? Is it integration only? There is a difference between integration and inclusion – integration is where you integrate all the kids in class, they have the

> chairs, the desks, they are all in class. Included means much more than that – they feel part of the classroom life, they are protagonists, not just spectators.

This points to one of the constraints of socially just education leadership identified by Capper and Young (2014) – the actual meaning of inclusive practice and the interchangeable use of the terms 'inclusion' and 'integration'. Moreover, this points to the lack of policy and practice coherence to address inequities. PH further critiques policy translation and enactment at school leaving age, expressing scepticism at the actual presence of a social justice discourse among the fifteen and sixteen-year-olds who fail the system (having been unjustly failed by the system itself).

> What about the students who didn't even sit for the exams? Is that social justice? We have an amount of failures, but we only boast about the success stories! Even if there are 90% passes, what about the remaining 10%? And those who didn't even dare sit for the exam?

Consequently, educators, policymakers and the general public are very much aware of the fact that despite this wide-ranging restructuring and reform, there is a considerable amount of the school population who are somewhat diverse from the 'successful' majority, thus falling by the wayside of the teaching and learning achievements rat race (Shields, 2004).

There is still more work to be done at both the school and national level in order to combat social injustices in the education arena. When probed about the changes envisaged for future leaders of social justice, both Heads outlined increased awareness as the major contributing factor. 'More child-centered approaches and pedagogies are needed ... there must be more awareness of the fact that every kid has the right to progress according to ability ... you do everything possible to help everybody move forward' (PH). According to SH, social justice awareness should be incorporated within the training and professional development programme of school leaders, since

> it is not an exception anymore, you have to fight social injustices all the time. Social justice has become the rule rather than the exception ... Students are being discriminated against all the time and this is not by any fault of theirs but because they come from countries with different cultures, for example. School leaders should be aware of these different cultures and plan for students with different abilities.

7.3 *Enacting Social Justice in the School: Facilitators and Hindrances*

When asked about their enactment of leadership for social justice in the school and the process involved in becoming social justice leaders, both PH and SH admitted that it is not a straightforward task, but one has to try, given the present circumstances and the current socio-economic and multicultural reality. This reflects Ryan's (2006) observation about leadership and social justice not being natural bedfellows, with their interaction very much dependent on leadership conception. PH states that:

> It is not a question of learning, but of being, you have to believe in social justice and need to put yourself in the stakeholders' boots – be it pupils, teachers, parents and minor staff – you have to provide opportunities to help the child grow.

The Heads' strong belief in social justice directs their daily school activities:

> I didn't learn anywhere … I look at a student, a parent and see what they need, one at a time. I hate discrimination and don't like it when students are discriminated against because of their background, especially if they cannot cope because of their low socio-economic background … So that drives me up the wall and I try to do something about it. (SH)

Understanding the 'gap' in a holistic sense, rather than solely focusing on achievement, in addition to dealing with deprivation and poverty, directs the Heads' social justice leadership practice repertoire.

PH, who is very child-centered in his overall leadership and pedagogic approach interprets social justice in a particular way that differs from literature's focus on the achievement gap between high and low achievers.

> It's not easy but you have to try … I identify some students as ghost students – these are students who are present at school, but whose presence is not felt. For example, naughty kids are the most popular, but what about the introverts and those who fail to stand out?

Identification and empowerment of these so-called 'ghost students' is his way of fostering social justice. He also attempts to foster this kind of social justice with staff members:

> As Head of school, you have staff, teachers who are bubbly, while others are very silent but still doing their job extremely well. So, you have to be careful to praise all, not only those who make themselves visible and are

the loudest ... Even with staff members, you need to foster this kind of social justice.

This particular Head of school knows each and every of his four hundred students by name, their background, giving them equal individual attention during their time spent at the primary school. He is utterly driven by this student-centered belief in social justice:

> Even during staff meetings, teachers know that my first priority are the students, staff come second, but they know that. My top priority are the students, obviously, I respect the staff but believe that the first priority of a school should be the students.

The sudden influx of migrant learners has added a new twist to the conceptualization and enactment of social justice within local schools, who until very recently only had to deal with 'otherness' in terms of socio-economic disparities. This is evident in SH's narrative of social justice leadership enactment:

> As a Head of school, when we are distributing classes, in every class, we have boys, we have girls, we have locals, we have foreigners ... there's a mix. It is not if you are a foreigner who has just come to school, you are put in the last class and that's that. We try to see the student's actual level of abilities in order to reduce the amount of discrimination that can crop up ... Students are placed according to their ability, not their ethnic background or social standing.

This stance is also mirrored in the practices of PH:

> For me, it doesn't make much difference whether a student hails from Victoria or from France, the challenges may be different, but they still find that they are part of the school. I can mention several examples of students who didn't speak Maltese or English, but then managed to communicate in English and understand Maltese after spending time at our school ... We give them all the opportunities to be like the others.

PH firmly believes that the students themselves at times create social justice more readily and adequately than the adults. He speaks about a London student with a different skin color who joined them for the last two months of the scholastic year in Year 6. The students did not even mention this difference, unlike their parents, but welcomed him and treated him like one of them. He felt at home, followed lessons, and even managed to understand some Maltese words. Cultural sensitivity is thus perceived as a core action (Arar et al., 2017; Oplatka, 2013) in the school's attempt to bridge the gap between the majority and the minority.

Both Heads involved in this study look upon social justice as an act of personal endeavour (Brooks et al., 2015), as they personally work on creating a socially just school by attempting to give every student equal opportunities and fostering this sense of social justice awareness among staff members. This unfolding of social justice is facilitated by the state-initiated policy discourses (outlined in a previous section) that are enacted in schools by the educators in differing degrees, in addition to the services provided by the Education Directorates within the Ministry. Among these ancillary services, one finds the psycho-social team, complementary education, reading recovery programs, the nurture class, the learning support zone, the Prince Trust, the core curriculum program, and budgetary measures that all contribute to combating social injustices in the school environment. SH is of the opinion that teachers are the main protagonists in the fostering of social justice: 'Teachers are the facilitators one hundred percent ... Some teachers are on board one hundred percent and these are the facilitators'. She recounts a particular example of three particular students with profound special educational needs who cannot sit for exams like the mainstream students but who are learning a lot of valid life skills. Their teacher made up a checklist in order to give their parents feedback in a different way. This demonstrates how teachers use different ways to cater for different levels. PH expresses his concern about certain members of staff and their role in the facilitation of social justice: 'Unfortunately, I am not convinced that all of them are doing their utmost to foster social justice. Some just cover the syllabus but do not bother to cater for the less able, to adapt their work'.

SH also voices this concern, as while pinpointing teachers as the main facilitators, they can also hinder the unfolding of social justice in certain instances:

> Teachers can be a hindrance sometimes. You think that a teacher can help you reach a goal, but they are working against you, instead. Some simply see their job as babysitting. When you have students who cannot perform academically, you need to see what works for them.

Other human factors that impact on the Heads' agenda to achieve social justice in the school are the major stakeholders themselves. Parents with impossibly high expectations may prove to be a major stumbling block:

> Parents have their own idea of what the student should be doing, and this keeps them behind as they can be doing so much more and they are not allowing them the freedom to do that. I understand that they have the

fear of doing something new which they think will be beyond the student who will then see it as a failure ... Parents don't always understand the way you are going about it.

Parents need to move according to the pace of their own offspring rather than in comparison with the other class students. Students may also pose problems, as according to SH 'you always have that someone who is completely unmotivated and no matter what you do, you say "I have failed with this student. Perhaps I haven't seen his real interests"'. SH further explains how foreign students may lead to particular problems:

> Foreign students may sometimes create a difficulty for our lower-ability students as some foreigners insist that you talk to them in their own language. Teachers have to code switch between Maltese and English all the time. Is this fair for our local students?

On the other hand, PH looks upon a major curricular issue that is centrally mandated as a hindrance:

> Another obstacle can be the fact that there is a common syllabus for all to follow. I do admit that there is continuous assessment, but still, everybody has to follow the same syllabus – perhaps it would serve better to be more flexible. The curriculum is becoming more democratic and inclusive, but the syllabus is still content-based. It has to be more appealing for everybody – the methodology, the way of doing things has to change, by introducing learning by doing in order to create more opportunities for students to master learning.

Consequently, this somewhat limits the social justice work of the educators in the classrooms.

In conclusion, the enactment of leadership for social justice depends on the leaders' perceptions of the social justice concept, as well as the facilitators and hindrances present within that particular school context and local education policy scenario.

8 Conclusions

There is a growing research literature on social justice as a key concept in current education policy and practice, as well as educational leadership in relation to discourses of equity and social justice. The inspiration for this project emanated from my direct experience of College Director in dealing with a sudden increase of migrant learners in a college network of thirteen schools. This influx of multicultural students within a school population composed of a vast majority of locals is a very recent phenomenon that took Heads of school by storm. With foreign students being viewed as the 'Other', I thus strove to lead these Heads into embracing discourses of equity and social justice while enacting them in their leadership practices with the various stakeholders.

As such, this study provides additional insights into the enactment of social justice within a policyscape dominated by education benchmarks in the form of high-stakes testing and accountability. The following are the main conclusions to be elicited from the study:

1. The Heads pursued a leadership position due to their innate desire to promote social justice as an educational goal, conceptualizing the term as the provision of equality.
2. Recent education reform has concentrated on enhanced quality education provision as an enabler for success. However, this very much depends on the teachers who are ultimately responsible for policy enactment in the classroom.
3. The concept of inclusion as it unfolds in class is problematized, pointing to the lack of policy and practice coherence to address inequities.
4. A particular interpretation of social justice is that of focusing on the 'ghost' students and staff, that is, those who fail to stand out from the rest.
5. There are several ancillary services provided from the state that promote the unfolding of social justice. Notwithstanding the fact that teachers act as the main facilitators, they can also hinder the unfolding of social justice.

I will now present the limitations of the study, plus recommendations for further research. Both Heads of School must be understood within the context of their work. Schools vary along many dimensions, among which are culture and community make-up, while school leaders' practices vary between education settings. A cross-cultural comparative study can incorporate schools from diverse geographical areas comprising state, church and independent sectors that cater for compulsory school-age education. This comparative study can also go beyond the national level to explore social justice leadership enactment at a European and Mediterranean level. The data for this small-scale study was collected via interviews from the narratives of the school leaders. A larger scale study may include the narratives of other stakeholders such as teachers, students, parents, and members of the wider community, thus yielding a more detailed depiction of social justice leadership enactment. The presence of social justice provision in the local policyscape existed before the widespread impact of societal factors that are now manifesting themselves in schools. Issues such as poverty and multiculturalism are very recent phenomena in local schools, calling for the enactment of social justice in order to provide all students with equal opportunities, notwithstanding their ethnicity, social background or religious beliefs. A valid study that would enhance our understanding of social justice leadership enactment is the extent to which the global policyscape affects local practices.

This study provides further awareness into social justice and education as it unfolds in the Maltese state school system. These case studies may be from a particular local context, but it is hoped that they can generate ways of thinking about and practising leadership for social justice across much broader contexts. In the words of Niesche and Keddie (2016),

> How they go about doing this should give us all food for thought about the contemporary experience for school leaders and the ways in which they must grapple with the current constraints of their work, as well as the spaces where they can exercise resistance and counter-conduct. (p. 158)

References

Arar, K. H., Beycioglu, K., & Oplatka, I. (2017). A cross-cultural analysis of educational leadership for social justice in Israel and Turkey: Meanings, actions and contexts. *Compare: A Journal of Comparative and International Education, 47*(2), 192–206.

Arar, K. H., & Oplatka, I. (2016). Making sense of social justice in education: Jewish and Arab leaders' perspectives in Israel. *Management in Education, 30*(2), 66–73.

Ball, S. J. (2003). The teacher's soul and the terrors of performativity. *Journal of Education Policy, 18*(2), 215–228.

Ball, S. J. (2015). Education, governance and the tyranny of numbers. *Journal of Education Policy, 30*(3), 215–228.

Barad, K. (2007). *Meeting the universe halfway.* Duke University Press.

Blackmore, J. (2009). Leadership for social justice: A transnational dialogue – International response essay. *Journal of Research on Leadership Education, 4*(1), 1–10.

Bogotch, I. (2008). Social justice as an educational construct. In I. Bogotch, F. Beachum, J. Blount, J. Brooks, & F. English (Eds.), *Radicalizing educational leadership: Dimensions of social justice* (pp. 79–112). Sense Publishers.

Bogotch, I., & Shields, C. M. (2014). Introduction: Do promises of social justice trump paradigms of educational leadership? In I. Bogotch & C. M. Shields (Eds.), *International handbook of educational leadership and social [in]justice* (pp. 1–12). Springer.

Borg, C. (2019). *Equitable education in Malta: An optical illusion.* https://www.islesoftheleft.org/equitable-education-in-malta-an-optical-illusion/

Boyum, S. (2014). Fairness in education: A normative analysis of OECD policy documents. *Journal of Education Policy, 29*(6), 856–870.

Brooks, J., Knaus, C., & Chang, H. (2015). Educational leadership against racism: Challenging policy, pedagogy and practice. *International Journal of Multicultural Education, 17*(1), 1–5.

Bryant, M., Cheng, A., & Notman, R. (2014). Editors' summary. *Management in Education (Special Issue: Exploring High Need and Social Justice Leadership in Schools around the Globe), 28*(3), 78–79.

Cambron-McCabe, N., & McCarthy, M. (2005). Educating school leaders for social justice. *Educational Policy, 19*(1), 201–222.

Capper, C. A., & Young, M. D. (2014). Ironies and limitations of educational leadership for social justice: A call to social justice educators. *Theory into Practice, 53*(2), 158–164.

Clark, J. A. (2006). Social justice, education and schooling: Some philosophical issues. *British Journal of Educational Studies, 54*(3), 272–287.

Connell, R. (1993). *Schools and social justice.* Temple University Press.

Education act amendment, Act 49-62U.S.C. (2006).

European Agency for Special Needs and Inclusive Education. (2014). *Education for all: Special needs and inclusive education in Malta – External audit report.* European Agency.

Forde, C., & Torrance, D. (2017). Social justice and leadership development. *Professional Development in Education, 43*(1), 106–120.

Francis, B., Mills, M., & Lupton, R. (2017). Towards social justice in education: Contradictions and dilemmas. *Journal of Education Policy, 32*(4), 414–431.

Gewirtz, S. (2002). *The managerial school.* Routledge Falmer.

Gewirtz, S. (2006). Towards a contextualized analysis of social justice in education. *Educational Philosophy and Theory, 38*(1), 69–81.

Harris, A., Adams, D., Jones, M. S., & Muniandy, V. (2015). System effectiveness and improvement: The importance of theory and context. *School Effectiveness and School Improvement, 26*(1), 1–3.

Johnson, B. L. (2008). Exploring multiple meanings of social justice: Comparing modern, interpretive and post-modern perspectives. *Teacher Development, 12*(4), 301–318.

Liasidou, A., & Antoniou, A. (2015). Head teachers' leadership for social justice and inclusion. *School Leadership & Management: Formerly School Organisation, 35*(4), 347–364.

Lingard, B. (2010). Policy borrowing, policy learning: Testing times in Australian schooling. *Critical Studies in Education, 51*(2), 129–147.

Middlewood, D. (2007). Series editor's foreword. In J. Lumby & M. Coleman (Eds.), *Leadership and diversity: Challenging theory and practice in education* (pp. vii–viii). Sage.

Ministry for Education and Employment. (2012). *The national curriculum framework*. Author.

Ministry for Education and Employment. (2014). *Framework for the education strategy for Malta 2014–2024*. Author.

Ministry for Education and Employment. (2016). *My journey: Achieving through different paths*. Author.

Ministry for Education and Employment. (2019a). *A national inclusive education framework*. Author.

Ministry for Education and Employment. (2019b). *A policy on inclusive education in schools*. Author.

Ministry of Education. (1999). *National minimum curriculum: Creating the future together*. Author.

Ministry of Education, Youth and Employment. (2005). *For all children to succeed: A new network organization for quality education in Malta*. Author.

Ministry of Education, Youth and Employment. (2007). *Agreement between the government and the MUT*. Author.

Mowat, J. G. (2018). Closing the attainment gap – A realistic proposition or an elusive pipe-dream? *Journal of Education Policy, 33*(2), 299–321.

Niesche, R., & Keddie, A. (2016). *Leadership, ethics and schooling for social justice*. Routledge.

North, C. E. (2006). More than words? Delving into the substantive meaning(s) of "social justice" in education. *Review of Educational Research, 76*(4), 507–535.

OECD (Organization for Economic Cooperation and Development). (2014). *About PISA*. Author.

OECD (Organization for Economic Cooperation and Development). (2016). *Trends shaping education spotlight 8. Mind the gap: Inequity in education*. OECD Centre for Educational Research and Innovation.

Oplatka, I. (2013). The place of social justice in the field of educational administration: An historical overview of emergent areas of study. In I. Bogotch & C. M. Shields (Eds.), *International handbook of educational leadership and social [in]justice* (pp. 15–35). Springer.

Oplatka, I., & Arar, K. (2016). Leadership for social justice and the characteristics of traditional societies: Ponderings on the application of western-grounded models. *International Journal of Leadership in Education, 19*(3), 352–369.

Reeves, J., & Drew, V. (2012). Relays and relations: Tracking a policy initiative for improving teacher professionalism. *Journal of Education Policy, 27*(6), 711–730.

Ryan, J. (2006). Inclusive leadership and social justice for schools. *Leadership and Policy in Schools, 5*(1), 3–17.

Schleicher, A. (2014, March 28). *Equity, excellence and inclusiveness in education*. Paper presented at the International summit on the teaching profession, Wellington, New Zealand.

Schraad-Tischler, D., Schiller, C., Heller, S., & Siemer, N. (2017). *Social justice in the EU: Index report 2017*. Bertelsmann Stiftung.

Shields, C. M. (2004). Dialogic leadership for social justice: Overcoming pathologies of silence. *Educational Administration Quarterly, 40*(1), 109–132.

Shultz, L. (2015). Decolonizing UNESCO's post-2015 education agenda: Global social justice and a view from UNDRIP. *Postcolonial Directions in Education, 4*(2), 96–115.

Smyth, J., & Wrigley, T. (2013). *Living on the edge: Rethinking poverty, class and schooling*. Peter Lang Publishing Inc.

Sultana, R. G. (1997). Educational development in post-colonial Malta. In R. G. Sultana (Ed.), *Inside/outside schools: Towards a critical sociology of education in Malta* (pp. 87–118). PEG.

Wain, K., Attard, C., Bezzina, C., Darmanin, M., Farrugia, C. J., Psaila, M., Sammut, J., Sultana, R., & Zammit, K. (1995). *Tomorrow's schools: Developing effective learning cultures*. Ministry of Education and Human Resources.

Whang, N. (2019). School leadership for social justice and its linkage with perilous politics. *Asia Pacific Education Review, 20*(1), 117–133.

Whitty, G., Anders, J., Hayton, A., Tang, S., & Wisby, E. (2016). *Research and policy in education*. UCL IOE Press.

CHAPTER 3

Challenges to Educational Leadership in Israel

Devorah Kalekin-Fishman

Abstract

In this chapter I ask how leaders' practices (linguistic, economic, and physical) create moments of autonomy and constriction to shape subjectivity in the organizations that combine into the Israeli educational establishment. Here I analyze regimes of practices in three organizations which are part of the system: the Ministry of Education, a private school (RH) where Hebrew is the language of instruction, and a public (accredited state) school (EM) in which Arabic is the language of instruction. The chapter is divided into five sections: after the introduction, Section 2 deals with theorizations of educational organizations and their implications. Section 3 describes how education is organized in Israel. Section 4 explores practices of the Minister of Education and the principals of two schools. Conclusions in Section 5 relate to how leaders' practices sustain models of organization while defining the scope of individualized subjectivities that can be coordinated with the totalizing vision of the state.

Keywords

autonomy – constriction – educational establishment – leadership – regimes of practices – schools – subjectivity

∴

Only the educated are free.
  EPICTETUS

∴

1   Introduction

By instituting education for the masses, the modern state has enabled individuals to access autonomous subjectivities but has also legitimated practices that ensure their submission to totalizing techniques of governmentality. The tension between education as a key to autonomy and its realization as constriction is one of the 'big' questions that elude unambiguous solutions. In everyday experience, the process is carried out in a set of delimited organizations each with a designated head. To uncover some of the intricacies, it is worthwhile to analyze performances of educational leadership in organizations with different functions. In this chapter I look at some organizational elements in the Israeli educational establishment and ask how leaders' practices contribute to creating moments of autonomy and constriction that shape complex subjectivities.

Among the organizations that combine to perform education, some are dedicated to imparting what is rated as basic knowledge; some are informal frameworks for 'enrichment'. Some are units set up exclusively for administration. Each organization accommodates sundry groups of classified young people, and clusters of grown-ups assigned to teach, to handle records, to deal with the surrounding community, and to see that actions are coordinated. Subtly, each organization involved in education is a community in formation. In administrative units, thanks to the formalized procedures, the organizational community is easily identified, if not delimited. In schools, the community is forever budding with the constant renewal of the student population. But in every unit, there are specific constraints related to demographic makeup and geographic location, as well as to laws and regulations, to community traditions, and to tacit understandings. In this chapter I examine the case of leadership in the educational system of Israel by analyzing what it means to lead three different organizations which are part of the system: the Ministry of Education, a private school (RH) where Hebrew is the language of instruction, and a public (accredited state) school (EM) in which Arabic is the language of instruction. I am interested in looking at how leaders' practices sustain models of organization while defining the scope of individualized subjectivities that can be coordinated with the totalizing vision of the state.

The chapter is divided into five sections. In Section 2, I refer to leadership as presented for practical ends and look at theorizations of educational organizations that imply perspectives on leadership. In Section 3, I sketch a description of how education is organized in Israel. Section 4 explores the practices of three leaders – the Minister of Education and the principals of the two schools cited above. Conclusions in Section 5 relate to how leaders' practices stem from and promote autonomy and/or constriction, to sustain models of organization while defining the scope of individualization.

2   Organizations and their Leaders: Practical Criteria and Theory

While education is often defined in terms of values and ideas, basically it is institutionalized and performed in organizations that operate according to some variant of the pervasive bureaucratic model (Weber, 1947). In the following I look first at pragmatic approaches to classifying leaders' practices, and go on to examine theorizations of organizations, such as *the new institutional logic* (Thornton, Occasio, & Lounsbury, 2012), *complex adaptive systems* (Drucker, 1992; Mitleton-Kelly, 2003), and a theorization of how *power relations* relate to the dynamics of subjective action (Foucault, 1972, 1982).

2.1   *Practical Definitions of Leadership*

An extensive literature on leadership promotes a practical view of how leaders' initiatives contribute to the success or failure, however defined, of the organizations they head. Focusing on performance in the field, analyses describe leadership practices in relation to the *structure* (formal array of leaders' tasks), *culture* (patterned convictions and conduct), and *design* (typical practices) that can be delineated in every organization. From this point of view, leaders in organizations, including organizations dedicated to education, are those in whom authority is vested to direct activities, to control the uses of resources while monitoring the normatively patterned behaviors that inform the pursuit of pre-defined goals, among them, for example, forecasting, planning, commanding, coordinating, controlling, making decisions and 'doing stuff' rather than talking about it (Fayol, 1949; Peters, 1987; Sarason, 1996).

Some models of leadership in the field divide the labor of leaders and managers, assigning each to a unique position in the organization. Ideally, true leaders are said to foster ideas, inspire trust, focus on goals, take risks, encourage and motivate those they lead to realize a common goal. Managers, on the other hand, are perceived to be those who control everyday procedures, focusing on the efficient execution of tasks; minimizing risks, and giving instructions; dictating the pace of work in the organization and following the rules (Leading Edge Consultancy, 2018). Discourse on education submits to this division as well. Training programs in Israel, for example, identify educational leaders as those with creative visions of the mission of education, engaging followers in long-term projects. By contrast, management is defined, somewhat deprecatorily, as an orientation to the run-of-the-mill coordination of 'household' responsibilities (Avnei Rosha, 2016).

In monitoring practice, educational leadership can, however, be operationalized as a fusion of the two roles in an enactment along three dimensions: *interpersonal, informational* and *decision-making* (Mintzberg, 2019). In the interpersonal dimension, leader-managers represent the character of the organization in their persons, are in constant contact with the staff and in charge of liaison with organizations outside their own. In the informational dimension, they monitor data on organizational performance; disseminate information about the organization; and in many situations act as spokespersons. As decision-makers, leader-managers are entrepreneurs, handle disturbances, allocate resources and are at the forefront of negotiations. Of course, decisions have to be made in relation to the interpersonal and the informational dimensions, as well as in relation to assessments and to policy-making in general. Given this description, management and leadership work together and can be demanded of every role incumbent.

2.2 *Comprehensive Theorizations*

While enumerations of role expectations can be helpful as guides to fulfilling responsibilities, leadership, and specifically educational leadership, is, in point of fact, a manifestation of comprehensive social processes. Here we will look at how it is viewed in theorizations of institutional logic, of systems and of power relations.

The *institutional logics perspective* (Thornton, Occasio, & Lounsbury, 2012) categorizes organizations as outgrowths of macro-social schemes. From this point of view, organizations are challenged to sustain structures of meanings that inhere in key institutions of the societal mosaic. This perspective proposes that the logic of every social institution is framed by: a guiding metaphor, sources of legitimation, sources of authority, prevailing conceptions of identity, basic norms, strategies for budgeting, and the image of the economic system as a whole. Theorizations oriented to the new institutionalism imply, for example, that a study of educational organizations within a politically bounded area discloses a constellation of institutional logics[1] which can be said to determine, or at least to shed light on leaders' responsibilities and hence on the performance of education (Kalekin-Fishman & Sharon, 2019). Whether or not they grasp the comprehensive pattern explicitly, leaders in education are profoundly constrained by the institutional logic and responsible for sustaining and integrating institutional meanings into the life blood of societal dynamics.

While conceiving of education as governed by institutional logics provides a conveniently fixed framework for analyzing processes comparatively, the implication of stability is quite misleading. As Drucker (1992) notes, in a changing world, the theorization of organizations must account for upset, disorganization and destabilization. Analyses based on the *systems* perspective can contribute to a broader understanding. Systems thinking considers that educational institutions 'comprise everything that goes into educating public-school students from the most general to the local levels. These include laws, policies, and regulations; resource allocations, and procedures for determining funding levels; administrative offices, school facilities, and transportation vehicles; human resources, staffing, contracts, compensation, and employee benefits; books, computers, teaching resources, and other learning materials; and, of course, countless other contributing elements' (The Glossary of Education Reform, 2013; cf. also, Fenwick & Edwards, 2010). An assumption of systems thinking is that all the factors listed – material, verbal, behavioral – as well as the factors implied by each of them, are coordinated in some fashion to shape a network of mutually supportive elements, representing the only possible version of active reality. But they are also the source of instability and change.

In dynamic systems, agentic action and reaction are inevitable; for actors constantly learn from experience and seek change. Thus, history, genealogy, and habits of individuals and of groups, are co-responsible for behavior in the present. As noted, there is connectivity among the elements, but control is distributed. Elements participating in action may be ignorant of the behavior of the system as a whole, responding only to the information or to the physical stimuli available to them locally, but every change is likely to echo throughout the system. Moreover, contradictions seem to inspire all the evolving action and only in extreme positions are new patterns of behavior and design created. As a whole, then, this implies that the system at once embodies stability and instability, as well as order and disorder, with coherent behavior arising from simultaneous competition and cooperation among agents. Still, while outcomes cannot be predicted, it is possible to perceive a kind of evolution in concert which derives from a constant flow of energy. Organizations are therefore often best characterized as complex adaptive systems where decision makers, designers, and stakeholders form and re-form systems as self-learning units (Chan, 2001; Cilliers, 1998; Ivanov, 1993).

The vision of school organizations as complex adaptive systems concurs, moreover, with Foucault's (1972) description of episode-conglomerations the socio-cultural significance of which constitutes the nature of organizational elements and controls their functioning. Given a social reality of constant adaptive change, leaders in educational organizations have responsibility for overseeing the endless chain of actions that emerge and recede, smoothing the way for accepting unpredictable evolution while realizing that there is no advantage to reversing the process, and, besides, that retreat is not an option. Delegated, however, to execute patterns of state governmentality, leaders are obligated to implement institutionalized styles of communication and to sanction physical constriction. In the pre-planned enclosure of the organizational community, the challenge that they face is endless involvement in power relations – acting to influence members' actions (Foucault, 1982). Techniques at their disposal include surveillance, rewards of approved actions and punishments according to a finely calibrated vision of how the system can serve the branded mission of a nation-state.

Every technique highlights differentiation among participants. There is on-going alignment and re-alignment among members of the community who are bidden to demonstrate knowledge, display compliance, conform to the sympathies and biases of community members whether positioned in the hierarchy or imbricated as peers. While they are rarely aware of the negotiations, partners to enacted power relations in educational organizations (students, parents, inspectors) consistently demonstrate their ardor for free action by raising banners of resistance (Foucault, 1982).

As shown above, comprehensive theoretical approaches to organizations have far-ranging implications for conceptualizing the scope of leaders' practices.

The next section describes educational organizations in Israel, a source of insights into how performances of leadership interplay with the state's comprehensive conceptualization of education.

3   Education in Israel

Before the establishment of the State of Israel in 1948, education in the area of mandatory Palestine was carried out in a variety of organizations with different systems of control. Traditional religious orders – Christian, Muslim, and Jewish – maintained schools for boys and young men destined for roles in the respective religious establishments. Under the mandate of Great Britain (1922–1948), government schools prepared cadres for the local civil service. Jewish schools that taught secular subjects were funded by political parties affiliated with the World Zionist Organization. They established schools where the curriculum and the procedures were designed deliberately to socialize children into an appropriate political orientation. When, with the withdrawal of Great Britain, the state of Israel declared its independence, schools of the General Zionist centrist party were serving about half the school population, schools of the socialist stream about a quarter of the population and those of the religious Zionist stream, the remaining quarter. But because education was relatively expensive, large groups of children had access only to rudimentary schooling (Tsameret, 1997).

Fundamental changes were launched with the establishment of the State of Israel in 1948. The mission of the 'Jewish and democratic' state that came into being was the 'in-gathering of the exiles'. This meant encouraging and enabling the mass in-migration of Jews who, it was understood, were exiled from their motherland almost 2000 years ago. At the time this meant promising legal entry and full citizenship to refugees who had survived World War II and the Shoah; and to Jews from Muslim countries. But it was clear that the 'in-gathering' of masses from states with widely different regimes could not ensure solidarity, nor could it promise that the population taking shape would recognize the legitimacy of the Israeli government. Thus, if only to counter possible threats to the newly established state, education became a priority.

One of the first laws enacted in the new state was, therefore, the 1949 Law for Compulsory Free Primary Education. The law obliged citizens to send children to school and obliged schools to accept pupils without imposing tuition fees. The promise of government funding unleashed aggressive competition among the diverse school systems (including promises of intervention in the labor market for the benefit of parents whose children joined one or the other educational stream), each determined to enroll as many pupils as possible. To overcome the chaotic situation, the Law for State Education was passed in 1953. This law provided for a centralized administration of schools throughout the country. It gave the Ministry of Education responsibility for credentialing workers in education, preparing obligatory curricula and assessments, approving and betimes preparing textbooks, for oversight of professional performance, as well as for generating rules and regulations *ad hoc* as needs arise. The Ministry has a central office in Jerusalem with subdivisions responsible for personnel, finances, security, curriculum, assessment, and so on, each with a hierarchical structure. A similar structure is repeated in each of the country's districts (Elboim-Dror, 1986; Ichilov, Salomon, & Inbar, 2005). Today, the Ministry of Education has a roster of 1086 employees who are directly accountable to subdivisions of the ministry, apart from the principals and teachers who work in the almost five thousand schools throughout the country.

Officially designed to do away with sectorial education, the 1953 law actually perpetuated many of the pre-state divisions and the variety of ideological interests are all still represented in the Ministry hierarchy (Lamm, 2000). In public education, there are divisions (with appropriate personnel) according to mother tongue and according to religious persuasion. There are public schools where Hebrew is the language of instruction and public schools where Arabic is the language of instruction. Among the Hebrew language public schools there are 'state' schools and 'state-religious' schools. Among the Arabic-speaking public schools there are differentiated curricula for children from Muslim communities and for children from the Druze, the Bedoui, and the Tscherkessy communities. Within the public school network, there are schools that were set up under pressure from local parents' associations; magnet schools work with curricula that emphasize sciences or arts; 'democratic' schools undertake to encourage children to choose their own ways of learning. In addition, there are streams of accredited non-state schools that have autonomous curricula but are committed to teaching what the Ministry defines as 'core' subjects, as well as an independent (non-accredited) stream of schools run by ultra-orthodox Jewish political parties where the secular core subjects (mother tongue, mathematics, English as a second language) are deemed out of bounds. Among the recognized private schools, there are schools that prepare students for an international baccalaureate, schools that emphasize the education of future leaders, and schools affiliated with Christian orders. Hierarchized sub-divisions of the Ministry are responsible for overseeing the smooth operation of all the recognized and accredited educational institutions. Since the state is committed to providing education for all, the Ministry scales differentiated contributions to the budgets of all accredited schools (Ormian, 1973).

Despite the heterogeneity of auspices among the schools, in the large, the centralized structure of the Ministry and its web of operations underlines the conception that Israeli education is a system with each subdivision designed to ensure 'latency', the maintenance of patterns of thought and patterns of behavior from generation to generation. In order to attain the goal of educating a solidary citizenry, the Ministry also deals with 'integration' (Parsons, 1951), namely, the identification and specification of what the state defines as civil traditions, cultural structures, artifacts and elements that shape everyday life that oblige all kinds of accredited schools.

Categorization in terms of institutional logic, a belief system that shapes actors' cognition and behavior, is also clearly possible. The logic of Israeli education as an institution is framed by the avowed goal of long term social control implemented by the state. Although there are gaps between sectors of the population, the root metaphor explicated in educational ideology is that of equity in the distribution of resources (Achituv, 2019). All actions carried out in the name of education derive legitimacy from the vision of building a modern, progressive *Jewish* state. The dedication to universalistic values that inspired educators before 1948, and was a highly charged political issue from the days of the first Israeli governments, is now frequently cited as integral to every aspect of education.[2] The comprehensive identity of the Israeli educational institution is embodied, however, in the slogan 'Jewish and democratic'. Education is charged with transmitting the essentials of this national identity. Although there are allowances for the legitimacy of non-Jewish education, education as a state institution is in practice guided by norms derived from particularistic Jewish traditions, on the one hand, and by universalisms that have been examined and found to be tolerant of the uniqueness of Judaism and Jewish ethnicity, on the other. For realizing educational goals, procedures and tactics are derived from the capitalist orientation of Israeli society, even though extreme actions are checked by loyalty to concepts of social welfare a core principle of the founders of the system. As is shown below, the concepts are regularly (re) interpreted to solve practical problems, and to accord with the party interests of the ministers in successive coalition governments.

In sum, alternative interpretations of the state's educational project are theoretically possible. Examinations of leaders' practices, however, can enable reasoned conclusions about how conceptualizations that are presented as iron-cast laws and procedures are molded into everyday reality.

4   Practices of Educational Leaders

To demonstrate differential conditions of leadership in Israeli educational organizations, I will compare everyday events and actions of the Minister of Education, a member of the government who is involved in the geopolitical policy of the state as well as in party politics, and those involving two principals in schools, the principal of a private primary school (RH) for Hebrew-speaking students, and the principal of a public (state) secondary school (EM) for Arabs.

4.1   *Becoming and Being Minister of Education*

While to become the head of a school a person must be credentialed as a professional teacher and undergo additional preparatory studies in management and leadership, becoming the Minister of Education is neither more nor less than a milestone in a political career. During the campaigns for the two national elections that took place in 2019, many politicians publicized their interests, and the position of Minister for Education was among the most popular. The appointment to head education has the double attraction of controlling a gigantic annual budget second only to that of the military (Israel Statistical Yearbook, 2018) and a presumption of having access to shaping children's consciousness (cf. Yanku, 2019a). Since the Minister of Education is a representative of a political party her manifest interest is to 'infiltrate', so to speak, her party's grasp of education into the everyday work of the Ministry.

Indeed, as the leaders responsible for the over-arching policy of the system of education, the Ministers with socialist leanings (1950–1977) emphasized the introductory formulation of the aim of state education and supported a combination of respect for physical work as in agricultural settlements (kibbutzim, moshavim) and in skilled trades, together with a furthering of scientific expertise, as well as cultivating relationships with Jewish communities around the world.[3] Since 1977, there has been more variety. With the approval of their parties, each of the Ministers (three from religious parties, three from a left-wing party, others from centrist parties) has nurtured some project that in his or her mind would mark a profound improvement in the functioning of the educational system. Each projected change was designed to revise the interpretation of one or another element of the institutional logic. For Navon of the Alignment (1984), it was of major importance to promote 'Jewish-Arab Co-Existence', a revision of the source of *legitimation* (Kalekin-Fishman, 1992). To this end he set up a Department in the Ministry, diverted significant sums of money for training teachers, oversaw the production of learning materials for furthering majority-minority relations, and promoted a new formulation of the aims of education with specific references to the needs of minority groups in Israel. His initiative came to fruition in 2000, long after his incumbency, with the Knesset's acceptance of the expanded aims.[4] By contrast, the Ministers of the Zionist Religious Party worked on reinterpretations of the *identity* embodied in the institutional logic of education. One introduced and funded TALI – Strengthening the Study of Judaism in secular state schools. The recent Minister (representing a more radical religious party) has made a point of introducing children in secular schools to the Jewish prayer book, and to codified Jewish laws related to government. Left-wing ministers reinterpreted well-established *norms* by introducing procedures to increase the rate of success in matriculation examinations for students in the peripheral areas of the country. A right-wing minister set her sights on detailed measures of accountability as a way of ensuring steady academic progress throughout the school system. Her successor, from the same party, attempted to rework the *root metaphor* by supporting activities of informal education, such as school trips, and interventions of extra-curricular enrichment programs to reinforce ties of secular sectors to Jewish tradition. Each initiative was heralded as *the* ultimate reform. In reviewing their accomplishments, however, former Ministers express deep disappointment in how their efforts were rewarded (Yanku, 2019b). They discovered that the actual potential of the position had been misrepresented. While they were appointed because of their prominence as politicians, and acted to advance party ideals, no political advancement was realized after a term of office as Minister of Education. In retrospect, moreover, the 'reforms' turn out to have had at best partial success.

A former Minister representing a centrist party, articulated the disappointment succinctly. Piron, who left the role after less than two years,[5] summed up the gap between the dream of being the Minister of Education and its realization. In his words:

> Those who want to be Minister of Education think that in that role they will promote the values they believe in .... They don't understand that most of the job involves curricula, pedagogy, and teachers' associations. They think that they are going to configure the spirit [and the consciousness] of Israeli children, but the "spirit" begins in gray routine. That is why those who get to this position are people who don't know what is expected of them. They think they will be able to advance their own agenda, but that is not the way things work. (translation by the author)

The deplored 'gray routine' is spelled out in descriptions of the Minister's everyday activities.

At work, a Minister's days are spent in series of meetings with occasional sallies for festive 'observation' in selected classrooms. At the beginning of every school year there are meetings with representatives of teachers' unions. Lengthy discussions lead to patching up the salary schedule, and once every three years to revamping it completely. These are the urgent professional problems that have to be solved by the Ministry to prevent repeatedly threatened strikes.

Throughout the year, most of the work week meetings have to do with a central responsibility of the Minister, collecting information and deciding on the form of its dissemination. To clarify the on-going state of affairs, there are meetings with sub-division heads, with the Pedagogical Secretariat, which approves new initiatives and collects information on proposed changes in educational programs, with the Council for Higher Education, which collates information on proposals by post-secondary school institutions that require discussion and confirmation. Another type of information that has to be collected are reviews by the legal department, and by the departments dealing with security. The Minister has to decide on the degree of urgency of each body of information and to approve the form of its presentation in official publications. Letters signed by highly placed officials distribute content that has gained the Minister's approval. Official weekly letters signed by the Director-General of the Ministry disseminate information for all 'workers in education', inspectors, principals, and teachers. The Minister's authority also validates timely 'letters from the pedagogical secretariat' that give information on projects and programs in the realm of school subjects. There are specific instructions that stipulate the power relations between the Ministry and the field, shaping the actions of all those involved in education. The terminology used is adopted to the referential interaction between officials of the Ministry and the professional as well as the lay public. The vocabularies settle into traditions of discourse and perforce combine to reinterpret the presumably inevitable educational goals so as to meet the constraints of the political context. Responsibilities for decisions and their publication as obligatory information intersect and constitute on-going restatements of the institutional logic. Problems of ascertaining continued support of the party establishment have little to do with the scope of the Minister's remit for educating generations of pupils. But in fact her interest in interpersonal relations is primarily connected with the party she represents.

In relating to the operation of the educational system, there are significant tacit understandings. The distribution of time and space are elements that provide an automatically renewed ground. In the large, the annual school calendar marking attendance and breaks, accords with the sacred and profane as laid out in the Jewish religion, but non-Jews have the additional privilege of observing their own religious holidays as well. Civil practices obligatory for all schools are also assigned according to the Jewish (lunar) calendar. Most significant are Independence Day, as well as two Memorial Days, the Day of the Holocaust and Memorial Day for Soldiers who have fallen in the Israeli-Palestinian conflicts. In relation to space, the architecture of schools, the divisions into classrooms, the equipment decreed essential are usually simply reaffirmed by successive Ministers.

In sifting the information collected by all the subdivisions of the Ministry and settling on the information to be disseminated and on its form, the Minister is in effect exercising supreme disciplinary power; effective governmentality is ensured by her designating unarguable boundaries of the taken for granted (Burchell, Gordon, & Miller, 1991; Dean, 2010).

By contrast with the comprehensive authority of the Minister of Education, principals in schools are tasked simultaneously with managerial obligations to carry out government instructions and with often overwhelming challenges in the interpersonal dimension. The complexity is recognized by the Ministry and since the first decade of this century, professionals who wish to head schools have to undertake formal preparation for proposing their candidacy.

4.2 *Becoming a Principal in an Israeli School*
In 2007 the Ministry of Education collaborated with a philanthropic organization to set up the Israeli Institute for School Leadership (Avnei Rosha, 2016).

Candidates interested in becoming school principals are required to complete a preparatory course in which they are introduced to six spheres of practices. In each sphere, a general statement proclaims the responsibility of the principal as leader. This is followed by an operational explanation of what the principal as manager has to do.

According to Sphere no. 1 the future principal has to devise an educational vision that 'promotes a sense of belonging to the school and identification with its goals'. Operationally, she is to formulate a work plan for the school and to show how she will secure its realization. Sphere 2 is that of 'improvement of teaching, learning and education' in the framework of which the principal is required to plan methods for teaching and learning, to develop plans for evaluation, and also to promote a 'caring, supportive, respectful school culture'. Sphere no. 3, 'leadership and professional development of the school staff', details the principal's responsibility for cultivating empowering relationships, organizing feedback processes for evaluation and at the same time, being sensitive to developments in the professional community. Operationally, the principal must develop viable procedures and institutionalized norms. For Sphere 4, 'focusing on the individual', the principal is exhorted to understand individuals' needs. She is therefore required to encourage teachers to be sensitive to the needs of individual pupils in developing learning units, to cultivate an environment that supports learning and learners while insisting on routines, and to collect systematic information on each individual's progress. Sphere no. 5, 'reciprocal relations with the community;' recognizes that the principal has to understand the ethos of the community whose children are pupils in the school, and in practice, to be in constant communication with parents, and to relate to the community at large making available 'cultural, spiritual, and social resources and infrastructures in the school'. Sphere no. 6 is dedicated to 'developing an administrative identity'. Here the principal is reminded of the need to identify problems in real time, analyze them and implement solutions, if necessary with the help of outside agencies. She is accountable for educational outcomes as well as for interpersonal relations, and above all, she is held responsible for conducting school life in line with the highest level of professional ethics.

The precise specifications, which cover interpersonal, informational, and decision-making dimensions of leadership, leave no doubt as to the type of subjectivity the principals are responsible for cultivating. The school as an enclosure furnished according to government models arranges people's bodies in an incontrovertible setting for the performance of education. The terms for principals' responsibilities indicate what depths of surveillance are legitimate and what standards are applicable for noting divisions among students and among teachers in the course of their careers. While the detailing of each sphere describes the heavy responsibility of the school principal for shaping the subjectivity presumed to be required by the nature of the nation-state, the inevitable limitations remain for her to discover in coping with the school routines.

In the following, I describe the state (public) high school (EM) in which Arabic is the language of instruction, and the private primary school (RH) in which Hebrew is the language of instruction. I will then note some of the issues that principals of both these organizations deal with in the course of a school day. As indicators of the widely different challenges each organization demands of the principal. I will then look at events of critical importance for the organizational identity of each school and for their heads.

4.2.1   The Schools

EM with its 400 students in grades 7 to 12 is the largest Arab public state secondary school in a city with a population of about 280,000. The student population is overwhelmingly Muslim, and most stem from lower class families who live in downtown neighborhoods nearby.[6] The school's internet site discloses that according to standards published by the Ministry of Education graduates matriculate at a rate that is significantly lower than the national average (40.7% vs. 68%), that there are no students who sit for the most demanding matriculation examinations in mathematics or in English; that only 38% of the graduating class succeeds in exams on studies of electricity, but 73%, a percentage equivalent to the national average, do pass examinations in communications. In regard to elements of school climate, EM is apparently similar to schools throughout the country in the rate of violence pupils complain of, but also in terms of the percentage of pupils who assert that they like going to school.

RH, with about 300 pupils, all Jewish, in grades 1–6, is one of six branches of a large private school founded in 1913 with a view to educating a Zionist elite steeped in 'Jewish learning' while emulating the culture of select European education. Together with the neighboring branch of a junior high school, studies in the primary school are oriented to the cultivation of sciences and art. Since tuition fees are high, all the students stem from middle class families from various neighborhoods in the city and from the suburbs. There is a highly sophisticated selection process which presumes to predict children's potential for academic achievement. In principle, the school accepts children from every ethnic group. But since instruction is carried out in Hebrew, enrolling Arab children of primary school age is generally not feasible.

On the assumption that the school's history as a uniquely successful institution is well-known, its site does not provide information on students' accomplishments in standard examinations or on the results of questionnaires that plumb the school climate. Instead, there are extensive explanations of the school's pedagogical vision, as derived from an ideology of Humanism, Tolerance, and Democracy. The site also describes the school's approach to project-based learning, its emphasis on cultivating technological skills, and its dedication to 'value-based learning'. On its site, RH also specifies that the school 'nurtures' staff members, promoting 'excellence, initiative, responsibility, team spirit, and identification with the school'.

Qualifications of the principals in both the schools cited are similar. In preparation for their appointments both have had teaching experience and have studied in the preparatory course of the Institute for School Leadership. The regulations posted weekly and monthly by the Ministry of Education are obligatory for both. For the principal of the primary school, there are additional requirements of loyalty to particularities of the school's vision. Both schools have an executive board, a staff of tenured teachers, some with responsibilities in the field of content, a counsellor, office workers, and a staff for maintenance.

4.3 A Day in the Lives of Principals

Observations of how principals spend their day yield similar data in both schools. A daily problem that both principals have to deal with is that of teachers' absences, some announced in advance, but most are morning surprises: seasonal flu, a teacher's child suddenly running a fever, a teacher who falls ill; and the teacher who suffers from a chronic disease and reports on an unexpected flare-up. Then there are the failures that arise in maintenance: the air conditioner that conked out in the classroom on the third floor (in mid-day it will be very hot, under the roof), the laptop that has mysteriously disappeared from the laboratory. A broken window – and nobody knows how it could have happened!

Both have to bring the messages from the Ministry to the knowledge of the staff. This is done by displaying the new material weekly on a bulletin board in the teachers' room. Urgent messages are sent to the teachers' e-mail addresses, and the most important points are reviewed in monthly teachers' meetings.

In the high school, there is noise in the corridor – two boys yelling at each other seem to be on the verge of physically attacking one another and pupils are crowding around them. The principal is able to disperse them. A program of enrichment scheduled for today has to be canceled because only two students of the original 15 are still interested. A teacher of Arabic says hello and points to her briefcase; she is worried because 12th grade students who have to sit for matriculation are still not writing acceptably in literary Arabic. On the desk of the principal in the secondary school are reminders, the one of a meeting 'today' with members of the staff who represent the teachers' union in the school. 'Tomorrow' there will be a visit by the district supervisor who is coming to check on how the new program in English as a foreign language for pupils who somehow missed out on the basics in primary school is working out here. The inspector will also be interested in aspects of the school climate as disclosed in the summation of responses to the standard questionnaire.

In the primary school, two children are sitting outside the principal's office, one with his father, who was called because his son ignored warnings and misbehaved on three different occasions; one in tears because a teacher insulted her. The principal will have to placate all of them. When the meeting with the parent ends, there is recess and the principal runs downstairs to the teachers' room. She has to see the counsellor before she goes into the second grade classroom and wants to make sure that the third grade teachers know where their pupils have to go for the introduction to robotics. There she discovers a problem in the schoolyard. The sixth-graders are not observing the rules and keep stepping into the play area of grade 4. She manages to delegate responsibility for monitoring the misbehavior and runs back up to her office to check some arrangements. Fifth and sixth-graders are scheduled to see a play at the municipal theater tomorrow and she has to see to it that the returning bus will get them to the mathematics lessons scheduled for 12:30. After 'the long recess', a new teacher makes an appointment to meet with her after hours because she feels that she has made a 'big mistake' in accepting employment at this school.

Both principals have to deal with stacks of monthly reports to inspectors and administrators on pedagogical issues, reports on problems in the budget, the secondary school principal to the appropriate department of the Ministry; the principal of the primary school to the financial official of the school network.

In this partial rundown of a day in the lives of the principals, there is little opportunity to demonstrate a capacity for leadership in the sense of an integration of the idealistic spheres dealt with in the preparatory course. It turns out that the everyday is best covered by the practicalities of Sphere 6. Quite simply principals are engaged in surveillance and in fashioning suitable responses to kaleidoscopic situations. Both principals are constantly called on to exercise skills in interpersonal relations, while handling reams of information. Only a few of the decisions that have to be made on the spot are related, however, to the detailed 'instructions' of the Ministry communiques. The peculiar mix of dealing with different types of unforeseeable crises and being accountable for creating a comprehensive educational environment are, however, experiential proof that in a school, leadership is irrevocably intertwined with management.

While the populations with whom each principal has contact are from different milieus, the modes of the encounters with pupils, with teachers, with inspectors are not dissimilar. But an examination of life in each of the schools discloses that the social context in which each principal operates positions them uniquely. I will describe two events that show some critical ways in which the roles differ.[7]

A chain of events in EM sheds light on the uncompromising socio-political constraints in which a principal of a state school for Arab children has to navigate. The attempt of the principal of RH to introduce a program that is innovative even though it accords with all the principles that are articulated as the foundation of school policy highlights the limitations of ideology and the contradictions that she has to find ways to resolve.

4.4   On the Conduct Required of a Principal in a State School for Arabs

Since the foundation of the state, principals of Arab public schools have had to act with extreme sensitivity to intra-state political currents. A chain of events implicating the principal of EM in 2011 sheds light on how central macro-politics is to interpretations of subjectivity in Arab education.

At the end of the school year 2010–2011, parents of pupils in EM wrote a letter of complaint to the Minister of Education (Nierenfeld, 2011). The then principal was, they claimed, inciting pupils and teachers to civil disobedience, and they were deeply concerned. A year earlier, when the preceding principal had resigned, a veteran teacher with an excellent pedagogical record and a background in activist politics had been appointed Acting Principal. As a condition for accepting the appointment, she was asked to submit a letter in which she undertook to refrain from all political activities. The parents now claimed that although she did indeed write the declaration, her actions throughout the year were oppositional to the State of Israel and that there was no alternative but to dismiss her.

In the letter the parents cited sins of commission. Despite a state law forbidding it, the principal had, they said, announced to the school that the 15th of May (date of the Israeli Declaration of Independence according to the Gregorian calendar) was a day of mourning for the Arabs' defeat in the 1948 war, the Naqba, and that pupils and teachers should not attend school on that day. She was also said to have instructed students to ignore the sirens that called residents throughout the country to stand for a minute of silence on the official Memorial Days. In one case, the letter stated, this was an act tantamount to denying the Holocaust. Moreover, she was openly associated with cultural activities sponsored by her party, and thus was still politically active. But there was also an economic side: she had, they said, hired only Muslim teachers.

With the letter the parents were making several important statements. They were announcing their acceptance of the majority-minority hierarchy in education. It was important for them to establish the fact that neither they nor their children could be suspected of non-conformism to the state's adamant self-identification as 'Jewish and democratic'. By writing to the Minister in this vein, the parents were aligning themselves politically with the government, distancing themselves from any hint of dissidence. Thus they were covertly insisting that there was no reason to suggest that the school's budget should suffer because of the non-normalized behaviors that the principal presumably fostered. Implicitly they were placing the principal under suspicion of support for 'terrorism'. More generally, the fact that they insisted on the principal's dismissal was a way of justifying a practice that was then in decline – that of having the General Security Service examine and monitor candidates for heading a school where Arabic was the language of instruction. Relaxation of GSS oversight of the appointment of principals in Arab schools was the outcome of lengthy negotiations with representatives of the Arab community. For the parents' self-justification, and presumably to protect their children's educational opportunities, they were willing to declare support for a blatant discriminatory procedure. What, after all, was not said, but provided a subtext, is that the territories of the West Bank were still occupied after 44 years (now 52), and although Israeli Arabs are officially citizens with full civil rights, they cannot be nonchalant about their status even within the legitimate (if not internationally recognized) limits of the green line.

Summoned to a hearing before the District Inspector-for Education and the Inspector-General responsible for state education in the Arab sector, the principal denied the accusations and explained her actions. But she was relieved of her position. Naturally, the implications of the 2011 scandal oblige the current principal to caution.

4.5 On Conduct Required of a Principal in a Jewish Primary School with an Elaborate Tradition

As a private school, RH considers the academic advancement of each individual student as its priority. In the school year, 2016–2017 however, the leaders of the entire network decided that it was important for students to learn about the meaning of 'living in society'. Each branch of the network was granted autonomy in deciding how to deliver the relevant messages. In RH, the principal and staff resolved to dedicate one lesson a week to 'social enrichment'. Children from the 4th, 5th and 6th grades met in small mixed groups and had activities connected with topics that the teachers found interesting. No procedures had been agreed upon. By the end of the second trimester, the teachers had exhausted their ideas for engaging the pupils, and everybody involved in the project was frustrated.

It was then that two researchers 'from the university' visited the school and presented a model for practicing 'participatory citizenship'. The principal, who realized that the model was an operationalization of school ideology, saw the proposal as a solution to an exasperating problem. Novelty lay in the model's requirement of redistributed responsibility. It proposed that heterogeneous groups of children should decide on some change that they would like to make in their everyday environment. If, as was likely, the group generated several suggestions for changes, they would clarify which was the most urgent. The procedures included: exploring the nature of the problem, going on to outline the kind of situation that was desirable, to plan activities that would bring about the desired condition, divide the relevant tasks among subgroups, and carry them out. Finally, the groups were to monitor the change they had brought about to see if indeed it had led to the improvement they sought. If the change was working they could go on to the solution of a new problem.

The ruling idea was that experience with the model would provide children with opportunities to acquire practice in reasoned discussion, as well as in collaboration, in reflection and revision, all foundations of deliberative democracy. As a solution to the teachers' problems, the model proposed to elicit ideas for engagement from the children themselves. Making changes in a well-known context would teach pupils what projects were within their power and what projects were beyond their capacities. An apparent didactic advantage was that the proposed model was actually a variant of Project-Based Learning, an approach to learning that the school had adopted and with which the teachers had experience.

But the introduction of a 'maverick' program created unsurmountable dissonance for the staff. The principal was working with people 'from the university' and dictating a change in an 'approved' pedagogical project. Teachers interpreted the plan as a threat to their professional identity, and settled into active and passive opposition. Identifying their selves with their professional certification and holding to the belief that teaching is an endless round of taking charge, they had no option but to resist.

The leadership structure of the school as a whole was another pitfall. In the network to which RH belongs, the hierarchy includes a group responsible for developing programs of enrichment, among them projects coordinated with the Ministry of Education. This staff already had a commitment to encourage community service, a highly 'social' mission that covered the idea of having pupils learn about being 'social' with minimum investment of school resources. The weight of the school's traditional design also precluded openness to relatively untried initiatives. In a network of schools burdened with a tradition of self-righteous achievements, the school staff had a footing for insisting on their right to autonomy and for resisting a transfer of authority to the pupils even for a single hour in the school's weekly schedule. Victims of what Senge et al. (2000) call 'learning difficulties', altogether the teachers demonstrated fear of being partner to organizational learning.

5 Conclusions

From this survey of leadership in three different organizations that belong to the educational system of Israel, there arises a complex picture of how the dynamics of power relations create and perpetuate subjectivities. Practical distinctions between leadership by the Minister and leadership by principals of fundamentally different schools are highlighted in the interpersonal, informational, and decision-making responsibilities that each leader bears (Mintzberg, 1989). For all of them, however, there is a clear definition of the scope of their power to order materials, communicate signs, and define how bodies should be deployed in the course of 'doing education'.

As leaders, Ministers of Education in Israel are responsible for maintaining the institutional logic of the state-generated project they head. Although many of them attempt to revise the status quo by promoting novel programs in the name of their constituencies, they discover that in the long run, their initiatives are likely to make for only small changes. In the realm of the everyday, they are involved in meetings where decisions are taken as to information needed and information to be disseminated. Whether or not acknowledged, perpetually renewed differentiations according to ethnic, religious, and political criteria are embedded in obligatory terminology of the flow of notifications. Groups are rewarded with recognition of their matchless distinctiveness and the sought for recognition legitimates divisions and re-divisions that are encompassed in the solidary self-presentation of the state.

Despite the highly different frameworks in which they operate, leadership responsibilities are similar for the principals of the two schools discussed above. The information disseminated by the Ministry in weekly communiques and in special publications such as teachers' guides and cautions in relation to seasonal dangers, is the position that they are delegated to carry out. There is no slack for avoiding Ministry 'instructions'. These maintain and frame models of organization while constricting the scope of individualized subjectivities. There is autonomy only to the extent that evolving actions can be coordinated with the totalizing vision of the state.

In the areas commanding immediate attention, however, the significance of the institution's logical obligations pale. Each principal has to be sensitive to the relational strategies of teachers, students, and parents, if only because they operate in complex adaptive systems, only sections of which they can control for short periods of time.

As the critical events cited show, the principals' exercise of power through surveillance and control of the everyday life of their schools is perpetually under review and often under fire. Conglomerations of episodes that turn out to have unexpectedly broad socio-cultural significance emerge to determine the organization's evolution.

The principal of EM has no alternative but to ascertain that actions of leadership are in tune with both the sensitivities of the minority community in the city and with the obstacles that the majority definition of nationhood presents to everyday life of the minority state-wide. In the background there is the looming logic of a sovereign Israeli (Jewish and democratic) system with overt recognition of minority rights and unrelenting practical repression of minority logic.

The principal of RH operates under a vision of the network that ostensibly stands for liberalism and democratic values. But the school population is enmeshed in a tradition of recognized successes that apparently legitimate staid self-satisfaction. Being associated with the school seems to indicate that subjects can command a luxurious ignorance of pressures for change. The certainty with which the staff develops procedures curbs aspirations to flexibility and adaptability, the very qualities that the school vision seems to champion and that the Ministry ostensibly supports.

By law and by conviction, leaders of organizations dedicated to education are called upon to demonstrate their radical 'freedom' to act. They are presumed to be able to formulate visions of the marvels that education can achieve while also managing their applications to daily operations. As we have seen, their attempts at demonstrating autonomy often remain unrewarded. The grandiose plans of ministers, like those (required of) principals, are constricted by the customs taken for granted locally as history, tradition, and morality. While the physical and temporal conventions of all the educational units in the country are consistent, leaders of different units have no alternative but to coordinate their actions with what has gone before, the prevailing tacit understandings that frame a specific site.

Ministers inherit the full weight of a legitimated institutional logic to which they find they can only add what are essentially marginal notes. Principals navigate in an environment that is constantly shifting – a panoply of competition and collaboration, stability and instability, order and disorder. The ideologies of leadership considered appropriate preparation for leading a school entice with promises of autonomy. In practice leaders discover that they are subject to the pressures of relentless currents of action and re-action that shape everyday experiences on the one hand, and those of a stolid wall of the taken for granted, on the other. Operating in a paradoxical field of agential subjects and submissive actors, both the Ministers and the principals find themselves tied to layers of historical reality and dependent on outcomes of antagonistic struggles.

The interplay of contrasts and contradictions that constitute an educational system made up of different kinds of organizations creates a dynamic evolving and challenging material, linguistic and behavioral reality. In the complex adaptive systems of educational organizations leaders are constantly engaged in attempting to shape the actions of those they are appointed to lead, but find their own actions inevitably shaped by the tensions between the individualized subjectivities they are delegated to convey and the responsibility they bear for ascertaining the submission of those they lead to the kind of solidary consciousness the nation-state demands.

Notes

1. Institutions relevant to education include professions, family, and technology which combine in different ways with the comprehensive, state-generated logic of an educational system thus producing variants. In the framework of the examination of leadership I relate only to the state logic that is directed toward governing the overarching educational institution.
2. The Law for Free Compulsory Education passed by the Knesset in 1949, when the mass immigration of Jewish refugees from Europe and North Africa was beginning, enabled a rapid expansion of the educational stream that was based on socialist ideology. The schools invested in the absorption of pupils from religious homes, assuming that it was a good thing to teach them a non-religious life style. This was expressed in secular dress, secular courses of study, and in ignoring religious observances in diet and in relation to holidays. A virulent opposition to these practices led to the fall of the government and a revision of the socialist government's approach to schooling (Ormian, 1973).
3. Aim of State Education (1953): The aim of state education is to base primary education in the state on the values of Jewish culture and on the achievements of science, on love of the motherland and loyalty to the state, and to the Jewish nation, on the practice of agriculture and handiwork, on training for pioneering and on the aspiration toward a society built on freedom, equality, tolerance, mutual assistance and on the love of humankind (Israel Pedagogical Administration).
4. The aims of state education are:
    1. To educate every person to love humankind, to love his nation and his land, to be a citizen loyal to the State of Israel who respects his parents, his family, his heritage and tradition, his cultural identity and his mother tongue;
    2. To transmit the principles [enunciated in] the Declaration on the Establishment of the State of Israel, and the values of the State of Israel as a Jewish and democratic state, to develop respect for human rights, for basic freedoms, for democratic values, for obeying the law, for the culture and outlook of others, to educate for attaining peace and tolerance in human relations and in relations between nations;
    3. To teach the history of the Land of Israel and of the State of Israel;
    4. To teach the Old Testament, the history of the Jewish people, the Israeli and the Jewish heritage, to transmit an awareness of the remembrance of the Shoah-and-Heroism, and to educate to respect them;
    5. To develop the personality of every boy and girl, their creativity and their diverse talents, to [enable them] to express their full capacities as human beings living a life of meaning and quality;

6. To provide a basis for boys and girls to gain knowledge in the various fields of science; [knowledge of] the human creations treasured throughout history, and in fundamental skills that they will need as adults in a free society, and to encourage [engagement in] physical activity and a culture of leisure;
7. To strengthen capacities for reasoned judgment and criticism, to foster intellectual curiosity, independent thinking and initiative, and to develop awareness of and alertness to change and novelty;
8. To grant equality of opportunity to every boy and girl, to enable them to develop in their own way and create an atmosphere that encourages and supports those who are different;
9. To foster an engagement in Israeli society, a readiness to take on public roles and to carry them out with dedication and responsibility, with a desire [to participate in] mutual assistance, [and to make] a contribution to the community by volunteering and working for social justice in the State of Israel;
10. To develop an attitude of respect and responsibility for the natural environment, and a relation to the land, its views, and to its flora and fauna;
11. To know the language, the culture, the history, the unique heritage, and the tradition of the Arab population and of the other population groups in the State of Israel, and to recognize that all the citizens of Israel have equal rights. (Israel Ministry of Education, the Pedagogical Administration, Rights of the Pupil)

5 Illustrating the political tensions that surround the performance of the responsibilities of the Ministry of Education, the Ministers of the Centrist Party, Yesh Atid, all had to resign from the government when the Party's head, Ya'ir Lapid was relieved of the position of Minister of the Treasury.
6 Non-Jewish middle class families, Muslim as well as Christian, tend to send their children to one of the private ecclesiastical schools in the city, all known for their high educational standards.
7 There are undoubtedly many critical incidents in the course of a working day that have an impact on the principal's practices. But the events cited here are each a chain of incidents and illustrate how the mode of life differs in each of the schools.

References

Achituv, N. (2019, October 25). Is Nathanyahu good for the Arabs? *Ha'aretz Magazine*, pp. 30–37. [in Hebrew]
Bammer, G. (2003). *Embedding critical systems thinking in the academy*. CMS conference paper.
Burchell, G., Gordon, C., & Miller, P. (Eds.). (1991). *The Foucault effect: Studies in governmentality*. Chicago University Press.
Chan, S. (2001, October 31–November 6). *Complex adaptive systems*. Paper presented at ESD.83 Research Seminar in Engineering Systems. MIT.
Cilliers, P. (1998). *Complexity and postmodernism: Understanding complex systems*. Routledge.
Dean, M. (2010). *Governmentality, power and rule in modern society* (2nd ed.). Sage.
Drucker, P. F. (1992). The new society of organizations. *Harvard Business Review*, September/October. https://hbr.org/1992/09/the-new-society-of-organizations

Elboim-Dror, R. (1986). *Hebrew education in the land of Israel.* Yad Yitzhak Ben-Tsvi. [in Hebrew]

Fayol, H. (1949). *General and industrial management* (C. Storrs, Trans.). Sir Isaac Pitman and Sons.

Fenwick, T., & Edwards, R. (2010). *Actor-network-theory in education.* Routledge.

Foucault, M. (1972). *The archeology of knowledge* (A. M. Sheridan Smith, Trans.). Pantheon Books.

Foucault, M. (1982). The subject and power. *Critical Inquiry, 8*(4), 772–795. https://www-jstor-org.ezproxy.haifa.ac.il/stable/1343197

Foucault, M. (2003). *The essential Foucault* (P. Rabinow & N. Rose, Eds.). The New Press.

Ichilov, O., Salomon, G., & Inbar, D. E. (2005). Citizenship education in Israel: A Jewish-democratic state. *Israel Affairs, 11*(2), 303–323. doi:10.1080/13537120420000326470

Israel. (2018). *Statistical yearbook.* Central Bureau of Statistics. https://www.cbs.gov.il/en/publications/

Israel Institute for School Leadership. (2010). *Expected outcomes from school principals at the start of their career* (3rd ed.). Avney Rosha. www.avneyrosha.org.il

Israel, Pedagogical Administration. (1953/1957). *Aims of education.* [in Hebrew]

Ivanov, K. (1993). Hypersystems: A base for specification of computer-supported self-learning social systems. In C. M. Reigeluth, B. H. Banathy, & J. R. Olson (Eds.), *Comprehensive systems design: A new educational technology* (pp. 381–407). Springer Verlag.

Kalekin-Fishman, D. (1992). *Implementation of the project: Involvement in the community as the basis for a course of study in pre-service teacher-training on education for democracy and Jewish-Arab co-existence in a multicultural society (1989–1992). Final report.* Ford Foundation, 123 pp.

Kalekin-Fishman, D., & Sharon, M. (2019). Citizenship education and the institutional logic of the Ministry of Education: Focus on early childhood education. *Studies in Education, 17–19,* 291–318. [in Hebrew]

Lamm, T. (2000). *Pressure and opposition in education.* Sifriyat Hapoalim. [in Hebrew]

Leading Edge Consultancy. (2018). Homepage. http://www.leadingedge.net

Mintzberg, H. (2019). *Management.* Berrett-Koehler Publishers.

Mitleton-Kelly, E. (2003). *Complex systems and evolutionary perspectives on organisations: The application of complexity theory to organisations.* Elsevier.

Nierenfeld, O. (2011, June 16). Parents of a Haifa school: 'The principal is inciting students against the state'. *Zeman Haifa.* [in Hebrew]

Ormian, H. Y. (1973). *Education in Israel.* Ministry of Education. [in Hebrew]

Parsons, T. (1951). *The social system.* Routledge and Kegan Paul.

Peters, T. (1987). *Thriving on chaos: Handbook for a management revolution.* Alfred A. Knopf.

Sarason, S. B. (1996). *Revisiting "the culture of the school and the problem of change".* Teachers College.

Senge, P., Cambron-McCabe, N., Lucas, T., Smith, B., Dutton, J., & Kleiner, A. (2000). *Schools that learn. A fifth discipline fieldbook for educators, parents, and everyone who cares about education.* Doubleday/Currency.

The Glossary of Education Reform. (2013). *Education system.* edglossary.org/education-system

Thornton, P. H., Occasio, W., & Lounsbury, M. (2012). *The institutional logics perspective: A new approach to culture, structure, and process.* Oxford University Press.

Tsameret, T. (1997). *Alei Gesher Tsar* [*On a narrow bridge: The educational system in the early years of the state*]. Ben Gurion University. [in Hebrew]

Weber, M. (1947). *The theory of social and economic organization* (A. M. Henderson & T. Parsons, Trans.). Collier MacMillan.

Yanku, A. (2019a, March 12). *Hit of the elections: Everybody wants to be Minister of Education.* Ynet. [in Hebrew]

Yanku, A. (2019b, April 4). *'The curse of the Minister of Education': Does this ministry 'bury' political careers?* Ynet. [in Hebrew]

CHAPTER 4

The New Public Governance: Corporate Leadership in Spain's Public Education System

Enrique-Javier Díez-Gutiérrez

Abstract

In Spain, the model for school management and leadership has moved progressively from a focus on democracy and participation to a hierarchical and managerial outlook. This trend was established by the conservative government through the LOMCE[1] education bill. This approach attempts to apply ideas and methods from the private sector to the public education system, with the intention that schools should be managed increasingly as businesses. This "neoliberal governance" is underpinned by three strategies: choice and competition, attainment standards, and accountability. These modes of oversight and management serve to "govern without government", inviting schools themselves to conform voluntarily and, in this way, learn to govern themselves following a set of rules established remotely. They are presented as elements of efficiency, both neutral and technical, to be implemented by "leaders" who must themselves be "efficient" corporate managers.

Keywords

corporate management – govern without government – neoliberal governance – new public administration

1   Introduction

There is a wealth of literature exploring the role that good leadership has in improving educational outcomes (see, for example, Berkovich & Eyal, 2015; Bolivar, 2012, 2019a; Crow, Day, & Möller, 2016; Day & Gurr, 2014; Firestone & Riehl, 2005). This pedagogic leadership is participatory and based on autonomy, commitment and responsibility (Connolly et al., 2019; Knapp et al., 2014; Leithwood & Louis, 2011).

However, in Spain, the model of leadership imposed is one that relies on a top-down administrative structure (Bolivar, 2012, 2019a; Saura, 2017). In this way, the traditional collegiality and democratic practices of directly elected governing bodies have been abandoned in favour of instituting a single-person executive – the principal – who aims to be an efficient manager (Bolivar, 2019b).

This is a case of "applying" ideas, methods and practices from the business sector with the aim of making the educational system function in an "increasingly commercial" fashion and where schools are managed more and more as businesses (Ball & Youdell, 2007). In this way, we find neoliberal economics progressively encroaching on models of governance and management used in the public education system.

For this to happen, a technocratic discourse has been developed. Apparently apolitical it is presented as something inevitable and necessary for the "modernization" of the education system. It's true political nature remains hidden as decisions on how to manage public goods are handed over to "experts" and technocrats as if these decisions were purely technical or "neutral" and did not adhere to any particular set of principles or ideologies.

This new paradigm of organizational practice is what is known as "neoliberal governance" (Ball, 2016, p. 25), and it is replacing democratic processes in education. This form of neoliberal management attempts to create markets in education based on the principles of choice and competition, attainment standards, and accountability. The function of the State in all this is the monitoring of results, leaving the key players to act autonomously (Moya, 2014). The new system of management operates through three main strategies of "soft power" exercised through indirect elements of government. The first is "soft privatization" achieved through the formation of private consortia, business foundations, partnerships etc. who promise to "support" the educational process. The second, termed "remote government" which specifies attainment targets and as such the educational priorities in place, using mechanisms such as standardized tests, accountability and league tables. The final element introduced to the management discourse is the "freedom-responsibility" dichotomy applied to the "autonomy" of schools and educational communities, but failing to provide sufficient resources and means, creating circumstances where they can "act appropriately" in a way that is "free and autonomous" and assuming that they have sole responsibility for the results achieved (Collet & Tort, 2016).

This focus on *governmentality* (Foucault, 1975), supposes it is possible to learn how to "independently self-govern". It teaches that institutions should learn to self-govern, subjecting themselves to certain centrally established and now deeply rooted rules.

These techniques of oversight and management serve to "govern without government". They are presented as elements of efficiency, neutral and technical, rather than as ideological and political options. In this new educational governance with its neoliberal slant, the most important thing is not the legitimacy of its starting point, based on values and principles, but rather the legitimacy of its outcomes based on the results obtained (Ball, 2016, p. 29). Effectiveness, efficiency, minimizing costs, short termism, competition is the new "logic" which has increasingly come to penetrate, to be lived and practised, shared and proclaimed as the new "normal" (Collet & Tort, 2016).

2 New Public Governance (NPG) in Education

The forces of neoliberalism, which have an unbreakable faith in the free market and freedom from State interference (except when they are in need of rescuing), is responsible for imposing this management model. Becoming ever more omnipresent, it appears in numerous reports produced by International Bodies (World Bank Group, International Monetary Fund, Organization for Economic Co-operation and Development) and, in the formulation of educational policy it has passed from the status of "recommendations" to that of an essential prescription to be taken by every government across the world (Moreno-Hidalgo & Manso, 2017).

They believe firmly in their own dogma: private management, which stimulates initiative spurred on by profit and individual gain, provides not only a better but also a more efficient way of managing educational centers and universities than public management based on democracy and the concepts of public goods and collective rights.

However, there is a large body of academic work that refutes the alleged benefits of the New Public Governance model (Verger & Bonal, 2012, p. 20), confirming its' harmful and radically undesirable effects within organizations with a social purpose such as schools.

In the case of Spain, many recent investigations (Bernal & Lacruz, 2012; Fernández-González, 2016; Saura & Muñoz, 2016), outline the adverse effects of New Public Management (NPM) which attempts to apply the know-how and techniques of business management, with the aim of supposedly improving the effectiveness and efficiency of services provided by the public sector, promoting a managerial style of leadership.

Amongst the negative consequences they point to are privatization, subsidiarity of the public sector, introduction of the client model in an educational context, competition between centers, performance management of personnel, cost recovery from users, etc. Of these, I will focus on those related to business leadership. That is to say, the imposition of management techniques on the public sector following a hierarchical model of leadership taken from the private sector accompanied by what is termed "autonomy" where this is financial rather than pedagogic, and accountability through standardized testing to facilitate a ranking system.

All these things are present in the LOMCE education bill (Bernal & Vázquez, 2013). Here, administrative functions, including those of personnel management, become the domain of a single individual rather than being a collegiate process. This principal administrator is named by the governing body, according to their ends. The school board is, thus, relegated to a merely consultative role with no executive power. The principal controls and dictates. Democratic and participatory processes are eliminated. What's more, principals are even given the power to contract third parties, be involved in activities connected with teaching programmes, and indeed, to select the teaching body, "establishing the person specifications and required qualifications for teaching posts" and "able to remove internal candidates from shortlists".

3   Effective Management of Educational "Quality"

This focus comes directly from the field of quality management, a model which was developed towards the end of the last century, that succeeded in entrenching itself within business management between the 1950's and 1980's, which uses methods of quantification and standardized categories aimed at assessing "client" satisfaction (Bautista, 2012). Given that the majority of businesses adopting these concepts were bureaucratic, meaning that, for them, it was key to have clear rules and regulations on how to do everything within the organization; or else they were highly competitive and goal orientated organizations fixated on objectives and strategies, their implementation was taken to fruition with this focus in mind. This being the case, quality management became transformed into a set of rules and quality auditing processes (Bolívar, Domingo, & Pérez, 2014).

The problem with this system is not only that it generates inflexibility, little by little increasing the need to define objectives, goals, indicators, improvement mechanisms, strategies, but also that it introduces distrust of the professionals within the education system and, in this way, the necessity of controlling and watching individuals and teams who then have to constantly demonstrate that they have completed the established tasks and that this has been verified and ratified by the educational administration (Brooks & Normoore, 2015).

All of this frustrates autonomy and distracts us from focusing on what really needs to be done to improve working practice. That is to say, the things that start to take predominance are quantity (Chiva, 2017) and the accomplishment of standards established in quality audits, rather than, paradoxically, the actual quality of work.

Effective quality management, however, has gone further still. The doctrine of the market as applied to schools has introduced a new component allied to efficiency based on cost-benefit analysis. Besides the fixation on standards and incentives and the verification of control, this model requires that every activity undertaken must be continuously assessed for cost effectiveness.

This model is far removed from pedagogic considerations. By placing value only on what is visible and what is quantifiable, the market model goes against pedagogic principles which need longer timescales. The solutions to numerous educational problems require decision making that takes the long view whereas, the market functions on a short-term basis and the solutions it produces are superficial (Aróstegui & Martínez, 2008). Under these conditions, education becomes a market commodity whose results must be reducible to certain "standardized performance indicators" which are supposedly a function of its effectiveness.

The issue revolves around the belief that effectiveness and quality in education can be represented through attainment standards, measurable through tests. This constitutes a reductionist vision – partly inherited from the positivist school of thinking and partly coming from the culture of efficiency and competition of the business world – which does not take into account the fact that no measuring scale or method of quantification can reflect complex social and individual processes such as learning.

This system pursues the increasing marketization of education, offering mechanisms of comparison necessary for consumers to make their choices, selecting between the "most competitive options", so that the market can function as such. To this end, politicians put pressure on schools to publish their results in league tables for the consuming public (as companies can be pressured to float on the stock exchange) and those schools which do not show a constant improvement in results are threatened with having their funding withdrawn or with being put under new, private, management.

The philosophy of quality management, imported from the world of business, has brought a whole new vocabulary to the world of education. Terms such as effectiveness, efficiency, productivity, competition, quality, etc., have replaced those of equal opportunities and liberation (Colella & Díaz Salazar, 2017). At its base, the fundamental preoccupation is that of "getting results" that are measurable and can be ranked such that the "offer" made by one institution can appear more attractive and create more demand than others in a merciless and competitive battle to attract more clients and receive more funding as a function of this. In this conceptualization of schools as business, it is a given that any educational offer only exists if there are families that "demand" it. Demand has now become the talisman for those intent on creating a market in education. This orients the politics of education towards the field of economics rather than that of pedagogy. The horizon of educational goals is reduced to the quantification of results in standard tests, the number of diplomas and awards achieved which is, in turn, related back to the investment put in and the labour needs of big business.

Ultimately, effectiveness and quality, which are taken as given in today's neoliberal educational ideology, hide certain vested interests that are, at base, politically motivated. These terms have been co-opted as a subtle instrument to make the official prescriptions handed down from central government, whereby control passes from traditional forms of bureaucracy to ideology driven technocrats, happen more efficiently and appear more acceptable.

This interaction also functions as a moral discourse which holds the educational community itself responsible for its own crisis and failure, calling for them to be more productive and profitable. At the same time it hides and shifts the central problems of education, particularly those associated with financing the education system, claiming they are problems of effectiveness and efficiency of said system. In this way, the question is no longer one of providing better centers of learning, school buildings with sufficient qualified staff with the necessary support; in today's climate, quality depends on how well individual centers are run and their capacity for attracting clients. The logic of the economy trumps the logic of education (Bolívar, 1999).

4 The McDonaldization of Schools

In this way, the neoliberal economic model proposes that publicly funded schools should learn how to manage themselves like private schools which are presented as models of excellence. Ritzer (1993) and Gentili (1997) call this process *McDonaldization*: school management McDonald's style.

We are told that funding can no longer be increased due to cut-backs in public finance and the reduction of taxes on high earners, or because resources must be diverted to rescue the banking and financial sectors. The first priority then is directed at "rationalizing" school administration such that its organizational structures, once democratic and participatory with the involvement and engagement of the whole educational community come to be styled on the "managerialism" found in industrial factories. The cult of effectiveness and productivity reigns supreme.

To do this, the paradigms of how educational organization is understood must be altered. The lead role is removed from the educational community to be given to an "effective" principal, whose function is professionalized and oriented towards a leadership model based on the management of finances, business and human resources. Participation is substituted by a pyramidal hierarchy. At the top of educational institutions we find dedicated managers charged with the efficient implementation of so called "modernization" policies, able to discipline and control teachers and the student body at the base. That is to say, the model is founded on "a great deal of vigilance and very little trust".

This pyramidal hierarchy of decision making does not foster a participatory dynamic within the institution, rather, the reverse, generating a demotivating, bureaucratic and authoritarian climate which destroys trust and collective cooperation. This is precisely the opposite of what is recommended in the available literature regarding leadership and structure in educational organizations (Bolivar, 2010, 2013; Bolívar et al., 2013; García, 2016; González, 2017; Navarro et al., 2016; Sebastián et al., 2016; Vargas, 2017). As these authors demonstrate, it is clear that models of organization that are vertical, authoritarian and bureaucratic have proved not fit for purpose in educational environments, including as regards the improvement of learning.

However, through the LOMCE bill, Spanish education legislation has sought to eliminate the small amount of democracy that still existed in schools. In this way, School Boards have become merely consultative bodies and educational institutions are now lad by a set of likeminded managers in charge of implementing the policies imposed from above as effectively as possible (Feito, 2014).

Whereas before the school leadership team acted as the representative for their educational community when dealing with Public Administration and would defend the interests of that community, demanding that said Administration fulfil its duty to facilitate the right to education, now, roles have been reversed (Izquierdo, 2016). This can be seen already in the bill introduced by the Spanish social democratic party (LOE[2]), where the principal is established as the dual representative – of the both the Public Administration and of the school itself – advancing the model where principals are named by that same Administration and who will, therefore, be the executors of their desires, becoming the middle management for this new hierarchy (Viñao, 2016). With the LOMCE however, this model of management went even further with power becoming invested in a single individual with control over personnel management to the extent of being able to personally select the teaching body. This naturally produces a bureaucracy that is both close to and dependent upon the political leanings of the Public Administration currently in office, one which is sympathetic to its actions, a disseminator and mediator of its instructions and aligned to its ideology. This reinforces an atmosphere of conformism and fosters obedience to managerial duties rather than trust in initiatives put forward by the educational community (Barrios et al., 2015).

The school system has received a veritable "terminology transfer", an exponential lexical inflation through a wholescale importation of management-speak directly from the business world: "total quality management", "knowledge society", "client", "marketing", "competition", "employability", "flexibilization", "excellence", and so on (Díez & Guamán, 2013).

Nowadays, even the training for entry into management and that which is given to principals in post, not only incorporates the notions and vision of the business world (management, competencies, balance, total quality, effectiveness, etc.), but also teaches how problems within the educational system can be read through the lens of private enterprise. The outcome of this type of training is that business has become the ideal to which schools should aspire and that the leadership team must become professional, specialist managers who have ever less to do with teaching and education and more and more to do with finance and productivity (Aramendi et al., 2008). This is helping to consolidate a "common culture" of management, thanks to common training and similar points of reference amongst those seeking these posts. Such a culture redefines learning from the point of view of profitability – as much in terms of the dynamics of the teaching staff as of the student body – impacting not just on their endeavours but also on their identities and in their interpersonal interactions (Ball, 2003, p. 91).

Without doubt, NGP erodes and in fact, destroys mutual support, collaboration and dialogue within the educational community, elements which, according to all evidence gleaned from both scientific and education literature, promote an environment which favours both the professional development of teachers and the learning of students (Moreno-Hidalgo & Manso, 2017; Verger et al., 2016). These elements being the very ones necessary to generate a positive climate of cooperation between the teaching body and the extended school community and producing teaching teams and organizations that can learn and improve, and indeed, sustain those improvements in the long term.

5 The Lie of Managerial "Autonomy"

This process takes place alongside a narrative that proclaims the necessity of decentralization and autonomy (Quiroga, 2017). However, it does not refer to an autonomy associated with the possibility of pedagogic innovation within each school, the adaptation of teaching and learning processes to the specific needs of the student body within that particular school; an instrument in the hands of teaching staff and the educational community within each school that would enable the application of organizational and teaching strategies adapted to the needs of a diverse student body. As Aróstegui and Martínez (2008, p. 112) ask:

> ... what kind of autonomy can really exist where schools have no say over the number or size of classes, or over the inspection system or the standards established to facilitate that system or the ability to replace elements of the curriculum with ones that are more sensitive to other cultures.

The neoliberal project uses terms like decentralization and school autonomy in ways that are both ambiguous and calculated such that through these positive sounding concepts it can introduce quite radically different meanings. The truth is, according to neoliberal ideologies, what schools are being obliged to take on is a fiscal "autonomy" lacking any guarantee of resources – economic or human. In a climate of radical cut-backs, the aim is to force every school to find ways of limiting their expenditure ever more and seek alternative funding from external and private sources.

In fact, during the nineties, the reforms that took place in the USA, United Kingdom, Canada, Australia and Latin America emphasized narratives that privileged terms such as choice, responsibility, effectiveness and decentralization coupled with a requirement for schools to function more autonomously. The result of this, "paradoxically", is that these reforms allowed central government to acquire greater control over the day to day running of those schools. This was due to the way in which the process of decentralization took place: without assigning the necessary resources. Today, after almost thirty years of reforms that supposedly increased school autonomy, central government has increased its power to determine school policies, curriculum content and evaluation processes. They have even created institutions with the means to exercise even greater control over school performance. Most worryingly, nowadays, what drives how schools are run are not educational principles or needs but rather the objectives of financial programmes aimed at economic and structural adjustment (Fischman & Gandin, 2008).

This is no longer a fight for improvement in education and the school system, of procuring more resources where they are most needed, of giving more support to those schools in the most difficult circumstances, but to promote autonomy as a form of competition between schools. A competition that grows and becomes more powerful due to the focus on results alone. Where schools in rural and outlying areas with populations containing minorities or those with particular needs, with few resources and high levels of temporary staffing which impedes the consolidation of a stable teaching body are pitted against those located in areas where the population is mainly middle and upper class and have good resources. In this way, the already existing social divide that we see today will only increase, consolidating this social polarization and destroying equal opportunities and social cohesion (Cañadell, 2015).

Competition between centers, supported through the league tables published by education authorities boosts market mechanisms whereby schools must fight to show, or sell, themselves as "better" than others, to show off their supposed "added value", whether that be in terms of programmes to promote bilingualism or entrepreneurship, facilities and resources, academic results, discipline systems, "innovations", or other ways. Families then have to fight to get into those schools that, in this market of opportunities, seem to be "best" – those that are placed highest in the league tables. "Because, in effect, families (above all those who have the most cultural capital) know that they are not choosing between equal schools but rather between schools that are eminently unequal. Unequal in terms of opportunities and environment for learning and for the rounded development of their sons and daughters. And here is the source of the lie present in many narratives: treating 'difference' and 'inequality' as synonyms" (Tarabini, 2017, p. 3). Some schools are free while others charge fees that make it difficult for certain sectors of society to gain access; because some schools have a diverse student body with pupils enrolling throughout the school year because of issues surrounding migration while others have a student body that remains practically "identical" throughout their schooling; because some have digital whiteboards in every classroom and others don't even have computers; because some have a stable teaching staff while others have a workforce of teachers that changes year on year. For this reason, as Tarabini explains, discussions that emphasize the virtues of competition between schools, the autonomy to reinforce individuality and in this way, differences between schools and the "freedom to choose" a school are missing the point that education is a common good and a right to be guaranteed to all and not a competitive advantage belonging to individuals to be exploited in a competitive environment.

Moreover, this conception of autonomy and decentralization supposes the transfer of responsibilities and functions from the Public Administration to each individual school and its teaching community in particular. Once this type of autonomy has been established, results are no longer the responsibility of the system nor of the Public Administration, but of the school itself, in other words, of the teachers who work there. In this way, these concepts hide a process of "privatization by the back door" of public institutions, in the sense that they no longer form part of a "whole" – the educational system – instead, each one is transformed into an individual entity that must compete with all the others and, in addition, capitalize its resources (exactly like a private business).

In this way, "programme-contracts" are agreed upon between Public Administration and each individual school or university, which individualize their particular relationship with the Public Administration, where increments in financial assistance are conditioned on the achievement of certain quantifiable results and where resources are provided as a function of results achieved. This not only dismantles the mechanisms for collective bargaining performed through unions on behalf of education workers, increases flexibility in contracting staff and restructuring their remuneration scales, but also absolves the State from its duty to provide the necessary resources and to guarantee quality of service while also allowing Public Administration to increasingly neglect the financial situation of state schools, especially those in most need of support and resources, leaving the responsibility for delivering a quality education in the hands of the "educational managers" (Carver, 2016). Thus, the responsibility for success or failure of schools is delegated to individual educational communities (Apple, 2002; Cañadell, 2005, 2016).

These strategies of evading responsibility, employed by educational Administrations, to which the design, planning and management of public education has been entrusted, tend to be wrapped up in the language of administrative decentralization, community outreach and participation of relevant sectors. However, while proclaiming increased autonomy, these processes are accompanied by a no less powerful compensating strategy of centralization founded on the development of national programmes of oversight and the testing of educational content (essentially standardized evaluations of achievement that all students are required to take); centralized curriculum reform to establish the basic content of a "national curriculum"; and the implementation of national programmes for teacher training that brings teaching staff up to date with the aforementioned curriculum reforms and their content (entrepreneurship, bilingualism, ICT, etc.).

In summary, the answer that neoliberalism finds for the crisis in education is a product of combining two logics, one centralizing, the other decentralizing: centralizing at the curricular level by defining content centrally, at the level of evaluation through standardized tests and at the level of teacher training (Medeiros, 2015); and a decentralizing of the mechanisms for funding the system.

6 Where to Go Next: A Democratic and Participatory Form of Management

We need to abandon the neoliberal demand for technocratic, managerial solutions to educational problems and face the fact, head on, that education is a matter of politics and democracy and also of values. We have to question the economist's logic of competition which dominates the political discourse surrounding education within the European Union, the World Bank, the OECD and UNESCO, and which, through "persuasive documents" seeks to subordinate educational policy to the demands of flexible workplaces, employability and the perceived imperative of competition.

To do this, we must work on three levels of participation: community (respecting the context of the particular school), policy (the management of the school) and academic (referring to the processes of teaching and learning). This brings with it a move towards an understanding of leadership that is far from the vision of a principal as the single agent of power, towards the adoption of a distributed or shared perspective. We are seeking pedagogic leadership that is capable of supporting teachers to better their practice so initiating improvements throughout the whole education system. This leadership should also be distributed, to facilitate the participation of the whole educational community in a joint project. In addition, we need leadership that favours social justice and which ensures that every pupil will receive a good education from the point of view of inclusivity and equality (Bolívar et al., 2013).

With regards to community, it is necessary to revise and put into practice certain concepts that have gone out of fashion before even having had the chance to make their mark on the majority of educational institutions: educating cities, classrooms without walls, open schools, educational communities, etc. and to give leadership for social justice a special importance. All this entails: (1) Promoting the formation of associations and the democratic participation of the whole educational community in school management – particularly pupils and parents – so facilitating a co-management of the school. (2) Recognizing the rights of the parent's association movement (AMPAS[3]) and student associations, promoting and regulating the obligation of Public Administration to finance and support these organizations and their participation in the education system. (3) With the support of Public Administration, foster effective co-responsibility for education, between teaching staff and families (Sugrue, 2015). (4) Broaden the range of competencies in terms of education within local government so that the provision of services can be organized in a co-ordinated fashion.

Taking a wide vision of participation and citizen-led management of education means that the neighborhood, the town, institutions, etc. all form part of the education process and channels must be opened to enable citizens to participate in it and for the school to enter social spaces (Crow & Scribner, 2014; Crow et al., 2016).

At the level of individual schools, participation in all elements of the organization can be established through the democratization of the use of space, sharing time, invigorating communication, designing, performing and evaluating shared experiences, etc. In turn this will boost a focus on distributed leadership (Louis et al., 2016) which, far from putting faith in the heroic traits of a charismatic leader, frames leadership as a quality of the organization. This implies the further embedding of democracy through projects and ideas that enable the participation of all in the running of educational centers: rotation of leadership roles and the structuring of these roles in a way that is collegiate and equitable (OECD, 2016); promotion of collective budgeting within the school, in such a way as to facilitate the co-responsibility of the whole educational community in defining priorities and deciding the distribution of public resources as a function of need and urgency as established by the School Board, etc.

Finally, at the academic level we must foster pedagogic leadership, or so-called leadership for learning, the results of which can be seen in tangible improvements in student achievement (Bendikson et al., 2012; Robinson, Hohepa, & Lloyd, 2009). This is because the ability of a school to improve its educational processes "depends in significant form on leaders who actively contribute to invigorating, supporting and encouraging their school community to learn and develop, so improving things progressively" (Bolívar et al., 2013, p. 20) by creating both the environment and conditions favourable to good classroom practice.

Ultimately, we need to regain a vision using the three big ideas now current in leadership research: pedagogic leadership or leadership for learning, distributed leadership and leadership for social justice, as outlined by Bolívar, López, and Murillo (2013). This means professional leadership centerd on teaching and learning, a distributed model of leadership where responsibilities are shared amongst members of the educational community and a leadership that fights against inequalities and for a more just society. We need leadership and education that are inclusive, democratic, fraternal, just, etc., in order to move towards a better society that is more inclusive, democratic, fraternal and just. In direct opposition to the McDonald's model which has failed everywhere across the world (including Spain).

Notes

1. Organic Educational Quality Law, 2013.
2. Organic Education Law, 2006.
3. Association of Mothers and Fathers of Students.

References

Apple, M. (2002). *Educar "como Dios manda". Mercados, niveles, religión y desigualdad.* Paidós.

Aramendi, P., Buján, K., Oyarzabal, J. R., & Sola, J. C. (2008). El acceso a la dirección escolar en las comunidades autónomas: un estudio comparado. *Revista de Investigación Educativa, 26*(2), 445–461.

Aróstegui Plaza, J. L., & Martínez Rodríguez, J. B. (Eds.). (2008). *Globalización, posmodernidad y educación: la calidad como coartada neoliberal.* Akal.

Ball, S. J. (2003). The teacher's soul and the terrors of performativity. *Journal of Education Policy, 18*(2), 215-228.

Ball, S. J. (2016). Gobernanza neoliberal y democracia patológica. In J. Collet & A. Tort (Eds.), *La Gobernanza Escolar* (pp. 23–40). Morata.

Ball, S. J., & Youdell, D. (2007). *Privatización encubierta en la educación.* Education International.

Barrios-Arós, C., Camarero-Figuerola, M., Tierno-García, J., & Iranzo-García, P. (2015). Modelos y funciones de dirección escolar en España: el caso de Tarragona. *Revista Iberoamericana de Educación, 67*, 89–106.

Bautista Martínez, J. (Ed.). (2012). *Innovación en la universidad. Prácticas, políticas y retóricas.* Graó.

Bendikson, L., Robinson, V., & Hattie, J. (2012). Principal instructional leadership and secondary school performance. *SET: Research Information for Teachers, 1*, 2–8.

Berkovich, I., & Eyal, O. (2015). Educational leaders and emotions: An international review of empirical evidence 1992–2012. *Review of Educational Research, 58*(1), 129–167.

Bernal, J. L., & Lacruz, J. L. (2012). La privatización de la educación pública. Una tendencia en España. Un camino encubierto hacia la desigualdad. *Profesorado. Revista de currículum y formación del profesorado, 16*(3), 81–109.

Bernal, J. L., & Vázquez, S. (2013). la nueva gestión pública (NGP/NPM): el desembarco de las ideas neoliberales con la LOMCE. *Tempora, 16*, 35–58.

Bolivar, A. (1999). Crítica de la calidad total. *Aula de Innovación Educativa, 83*, 78–82.

Bolívar, A. (2010). El liderazgo educativo y su papel en la mejora: Una revisión actual de sus posibilidades y limitaciones. *Psicoperspectivas, 9*(2), 9–33.

Bolívar, A. (2012). *Políticas actuales de mejora y liderazgo educativo*. Aljibe.

Bolívar, A. (2013). Cambio y liderazgo educativo en tiempos de crisis. *Organización y gestión educativa: Revista del Fórum Europeo de Administradores de la Educación, 21*(4), 14–17.

Bolívar, A. (2019a). Políticas de Gestión Escolar desde una Perspectiva Comparada: La "Excepción Ibérica". *Economía de la Educación y Política Educativa, 910*, 93–103. https://doi.org/10.32796/ice.2019.910.6916

Bolívar, A. (2019b). *Una dirección escolar con capacidad de liderazgo pedagógico*. La Muralla.

Bolívar, A., Domingo, J., & Pérez García, P. (2014). Crisis and reconstruction of teachers' professional identity: The case of secondary school teachers in Spain. *The Open Sports Sciences Journal, 7*, 106–112. https://doi.org/10.2174/1875399X01407010106

Bolívar, A., López Yáñez, J., & Murillo, J. (2013). Liderazgo en las instituciones educativas. Una revisión de líneas de investigación. *Fuentes, 14*, 15–60.

Brooks, J., & Normore, A. (2015). Qualitative research and educational leadership. *International Journal of Educational Management, 29*(7), 798–806. https://doi.org/10.1108/ijem-06-2015-0083

Cañadell, R. (2005). El debate oculto sobre la educación. *Cuadernos de Pedagogía, 346*, 82–86.

Cañadell, R. (2015). De la protesta a la propuesta: Una ILP para un nuevo sistema educativo en Cataluña. *El Viejo topo, 326*, 48–55.

Cañadell, R. (2016). La lucha educa. Movimientos sociales y renovación pedagógica: Educación, lucha y transformación social. *Viento sur: Por una izquierda alternativa, 147*, 47–55.

Carver, C. L. (2016). Transforming identities: The transition from teacher to leader during teacher leader preparation. *Journal of Research on Leadership Education, 11*(2), 158–180. https://doi.org/10.1177/1942775116658635

Chiva Gómez, R. (2017, June 11). La gestión de la calidad o cómo acabar con la Universidad lentamente. *El Diario.es*. https://goo.gl/t5AJkQ

Colella, L., & Díaz Salazar, R. (2017). Análisis de la calidad educativa en el discurso neoliberal. *Educar, 53*(2), 447–465.

Collet, J., & Tort, A. (Eds.). (2016). *La Gobernanza Escolar*. Morata.

Crow, G. M., Day, C., & Møller, J. (2016). Framing research on school principals' identities. *International Journal of Leadership in Education*. http://dx.doi.org/10.1080/13603124.2015.1123299

Crow, G. M., & Scribner, M. P. S. (2014). Professional identities of urban school leaders. In H. R. Milner & K. Lomotey (Eds.), *Handbook of urban education* (pp. 287–304). Routledge Press.

Day, C., & Gurr, D. (Eds.). (2014). *Leading schools successfully: Stories from the field*. Routledge.

Díez Gutiérrez, E. J., & Guamán, A. (Eds.). (2013). *Educación pública: de tod@s para tod@s. Las claves de la "marea verde"*. Bomarzo.

Feito, R. (2014). Treinta años de Consejos Escolares: la participación de los padres y de las madres en el control y gestión de los centros sostenidos con fondos públicos. *Profesorado. Revista de Currículum y Formación del Profesorado, 18*(2), 51–67.

Fernández-González, N. (2016). Repensando las políticas de privatización en educación: El cercamiento de la escuela. *Archivos Analíticos de Políticas Educativas, 24*(123), 36–44.

Firestone, W., & Riehl, C. (Eds.). (2005). *A new agenda: Directions for research on educational leadership*. Teachers College Press.

Fischman, G. E., & Gandin, L. A. (2008). Escola Cidada y los discursos críticos de esperanza educativa. In P. McLaren & J. L. Kincheloe (Eds.), *Pedagogía crítica. De qué hablamos, dónde estamos* (pp. 287–304). Graó.

Foucault, M. (1975). *Vigilar y Castigar*. Ediciones Siglo XXI.

García Garnica, M. (2016). *Dirección pedagógica y liderazgo educativo: prácticas eficaces en centros públicos andaluces* (Doctoral dissertation). Universidad de Granada, Digibug. https://digibug.ugr.es/handle/10481/43400

Gentili, P. (1997). *Cultura, política y currículo. Ensayos sobre la crisis de la escuela pública*. Losada.

González González, M. T. (2017). La dirección del centro escolar y el liderazgo pedagógico. *Revista Padres y Maestros, 370*, 6–11.

Izquierdo Gómez, D. (2016). ¿Qué hacen los directores de centros escolares? Las prácticas de dirección en España a partir de los estudios internacionales PISA y TALIS. *Revista Complutense de Educación, 27*(3), 1193–1209.

Knapp, M. S., Honig, M. I., Plecki, M. L., Portin, B. S., & Copland, M. A. (2014). *Learning-focused leadership in action: Improving instruction in schools and districts*. Routledge.

Leithwood, K., & Louis, K. S. (Eds.). (2011). *Linking leadership to student learning*. Jossey-Bass.

Louis, K. S., Murphy, J., & Smylie, M. (2016). Caring leadership in schools: Findings from exploratory analysis. *Educational Administration Quarterly, 52*(2), 310–340. https://doi.org/10.1177/0013161X15627678

Medeiros Dos Santos, S. H. D. (2015). Políticas de formación docente para la educación profesional: oposiciones y permanencias marcados por el ideario neoliberal. *Acta Scientiarum. Education, 37*(2), 165–175.

Moreno-Hidalgo, M., & Manso, J. (2017). La Nueva Gestión de lo Público (NGP) como tendencia educativa global y su impacto en la conformación de la identidad docente. *RIESED Revista Internacional de Estudios sobre Sistemas Educativos, 2*(7), 33–51.

Moya Otero, J. (2014). *La ideología del esfuerzo*. Catarata.

Navarro Weckmann, M. A., Guzmán Ibarra, I., & Guaderrama Martínez, X. R. (2016). Una mirada sobre la dirección escolar. In J. L. Bernal Agudo (Ed.), *Globalización y organizaciones educativas: Comunicaciones* (pp. 323–330). CIOIE.

OECD. (2016). *School leadership for learning: Insights from TALIS 2013.* Author. http://dx.doi.org/10.1787/9789264258341-en

Quiroga, A. R. (2017). Escuela y producción de subjetividad. El papel de la educación en las sociedades del gerenciamiento y el paradigma de la gestión escolar. *Ixtli. Revista Latinoamericana de Filosofía de la Educación, 4*(8), 221–235.

Ritzer, G. (1993). *The McDonaldization of society: An investigation into the changing character of contemporary social life.* Pine Forge Press.

Robinson, V., Hohepa, M., & Lloyd, C. (2009). *School leadership and student outcomes: Identifying what works and why: Best Evidence Synthesis iteration (BES).* Ministry of Education.

Saura, G. (2017). ¿Crisis? ¿Qué crisis? Filantrocapitalismo, neoliberalización y gobernanza en la política educativa global. *Nuestra Bandera, 236,* 32–43.

Saura, G., & Muñoz, J. L. (2016). Prácticas neoliberales de endo-privatización y nuevas formas de resistencia colectiva en el contexto de la política educativa española. *Revista Educación, Política y Sociedad, 1*(2), 43–72.

Sebastián Heredero, E., Catalán Cueto, J. P., Herrera, F., Utrera Infantes, C., Acosta Vargas, J. S., & Martín Bris, M. (2016). El liderazgo en la dirección y gestión para instituciones educativas en España e Iberoamérica. In J. L. Bernal Agudo (Ed.), *Globalización y organizaciones educativas: Libro de Simposios* (pp. 70–103). CIOIE.

Sugrue, C. (2015). *Unmasking school leadership: A longitudinal life history of school leaders.* Springer. https://doi.org/10.1007/978-94-017-9433-6

Tarabini, A. (2017, March 21). De nuevo con la elección escolar: o cuando la diferencia se confunde con la desigualdad. *El diario de la Educación.* https://goo.gl/9o9bTq

Vargas Jiménez, I. (2017). Mirada de la comunidad educativa acerca del desempeño de directivas educativas: Algunas reflexiones. *Revista Electrónica Educare, 21*(1), 1–7.

Verger, A., & Bonal, X. (2012). La emergencia de las alianzas público-privado en la agenda educativa global: nuevos retos para la investigación educativa. *Profesorado. Revista de currículum y formación del profesorado, 16*(3), 11–29.

Verger, A., Bonal, X., & Zancajo, A. (2016). Recontextualización de políticas y (cuasi) mercados educativos. Un análisis de las dinámicas de demanda y oferta escolar en chile. *Archivos Analíticos de Políticas Educativas, 24*(27), 42–54.

Viñao, A. (2016). El modelo neoconservador de gobernanza escolar: Principios, estrategias y consecuencias en España. In J. Collet & A. Tort (Eds.), *La Gobernanza Escolar* (pp. 41–64). Morata.

CHAPTER 5

School Leadership within a Centralized Education System: A Success Story from Cyprus through a Decade of Research

Petros Pashiardis and Antonios Kafa

Abstract

Based on the practicing of successful school leadership, both at the primary as well as the secondary level of education, within the centralized education system of Cyprus, we present the findings from a ten-year research project. Specifically, through an original qualitative empirical research study, undertaken through the examination of eleven case studies of successful primary and secondary school leaders, the findings indicate that successful school leadership in Cyprus is practiced through the combination of particular professional and personal attributes that affect and/or interact with the internal and the external dimensions of a school organization. Specifically, based on this internal and external dimensions, successful school leaders exhibit the following characteristics: (1) Networked Leadership – Developing external relations, (2) People-centered leadership – Shared ownership and collaborative commitment and (3) Clear vision and values. Additionally, based on this study, we argue that school leadership is also highly contextualized and we support the notion that school leaders' preparation programs should be context-based and context-specific.

Keywords

school leadership – Cyprus – centralized education system – successful school leaders

1 Introduction

There is no doubt that school leadership is considered to be an important factor for school effectiveness, due to the changing context of education across the world (Pashiardis & Johansson, 2016). Indeed, this is also evident through the existence of the research interest in school leadership, as an indication of the strong relation between the concepts of school leadership and school success and effectiveness. Additionally, this research interest highlights the important role of school leaders, as a central pillar in the establishment of a school organization's improvement process. However, two decades ago the orientation on school leadership research, in most cases, aimed to the school characteristics as an organization rather than focusing on the successful school leaders who led those schools (Jacobson & Day, 2007). Central to this discussion, is the fact that up until today the challenge of research in the field of educational leadership is to set up the framework and conceptualize the characteristics of successful school leaders as change agents in school organizations, especially in the Central European context, since a large number of the literature in this particular topic was derived from studies in North America and the United Kingdom (Gurr, 2015). Based on this assumption, several studies have examined school leaders' roles and provided clear evidence on what school leaders do and do not do in relation to change and success (e.g. Gurr, Drysdale, Longmuir, & McCrohan, 2018; Pashiardis, Brauckmann, & Kafa, 2018a; Pashiardis, Brauckmann, & Kafa, 2018b; Day, Gu, & Sammons, 2016; Wang, Gurr, Drysdale, 2016; Pashiardis, Savvides, & Lytra, 2011; Pashiardis, Kafa, & Marmara, 2012; Elmore, 2000; Newmann, King, & Youngs, 2000; Fullan, 2001; McLaughlin & Talbert, 2001).

Moreover, at an international level, research has been conducted on the key qualities, skills and behaviors central to successful school principalship (e.g. Day & Leithwood, 2007; Jacobson Johnsov, Ylimaki, & Giles, 2005). These studies indicated that successful school leaders possess, retain and communicate in all that they do and say, a strong sense of agency, core sets of deeply held values, moral and ethical purposes and immense amounts of emotional understandings of themselves and others. It is equally clear that they work long hours, are totally committed, have a clear, well-articulated sense of purpose and individual identity, are able to build and sustain individual and collective capabilities; are deeply respected and trusted by the communities which they serve; and are persistently resilient. Significantly, school leaders display critical assertiveness rather than compliancy in response to the sustained externally imposed reformist cultures in which they and their colleagues work. They are also able to manage a number of agendas, without themselves becoming negative and are able to maintain hope and hopefulness.

However, the meaning of successful school leadership must be seen in relation to the context in which the various stakeholders are located and the values underpinning the school as an institution in each society (Dimmock & Walker, 2000). As a consequence, the research interest that remains strong up to this day, is focused on how school leadership emerges and operates in diverse contexts and cultures across the world. In addition, Brauckmann and Pashiardis (2011) formulated a framework with five different leadership styles/areas that school leaders are likely to employ during their leadership practice (see also Pashiardis, 2014). Specifically, these five leadership styles/areas are as follows: Instructional style (strong focus on the improvement of the quality of teaching and learning), Structuring style (aspects of providing clarity, direction and coordination to the school), Participative style (school leaders can organize their management activities through others in many different ways), Entrepreneurial style (creation of external networks and alliances in order to enhance the implementation of the school's mission), and Personnel development style (when school leaders provide professional growth opportunities for their personnel). According to Brauckmann and Pashiardis (2011), successful school leaders are those who select particular practices derived from the five aforementioned leadership styles and create their own "cocktail leadership mix". Based on this, it is clearly stated that a school leader promotes different practices from different leadership styles that include the collaboration of both the internal and external school stakeholders and taking into consideration the specific context in which his/her school is situated.

Thus, it is very crucial to understand those contextual factors that could be located at the system level or at the school level and can influence the action radius, the array of tasks, and the prioritising of tasks that school leaders perform (Brauckmann & Pashiardis, 2011). Brauckmann and Pashiardis (2008) stress that there is no single model of successful school leadership which could be easily transferred across the different school-level and system-level contexts. What's more on that, is the fact that we have to take into consideration that policy initiatives that work well in one country could not, necessarily, be transferred across other national borders (Pashiardis & Brauckmann, 2009). As a result, school leadership is highly contextualized not only at the system level, but also at the school level. More precisely, a school leader would be wise to look at the situation/environment of his/her particular school context, whether a school is rural or urban, high or low performing etc. and then act on it. Based on the aforementioned, we present the results from a ten-year research work with regards to successful school leadership in Cyprus, both at the primary as well as the secondary levels of education (see Pashiardis et al., 2011, 2012) in an effort to provide scientific data on how successful school leaders perform their duties at their respective school organizations within the Cyprus context. This overall effort will be positively contributing to the knowledge of the existing body of research with regards to the International Successful School Principalship Project (ISSPP) project as well as to the literature pool on Cyprus' successful school leadership. Furthermore, the presented results of the Cypriot case will enable readers to compare, interact and add to the results of other successful school leadership contexts.

2   The Cyprus Educational Context

Firstly, it is important to provide a broad description of the context in which the study took place. As was stated above, the study of effective and successful school leadership is conceptually determined by the research data we collect from the various contexts in which they operate. Based on this information, together with the research results, we can provide concrete conclusions about the conceptualization of successful school leadership within the context of Cyprus. The island of Cyprus is the third largest island in the Mediterranean Sea. Specifically, it is situated in the north-eastern part, 380 km north of Egypt, 105 km west of Syria, 75 km south of Turkey, and 380 km east of the nearest Greek island, Rhodes. In 1960, Cyprus gained its independence and became an independent state. The constitution of Cyprus recognizes Greek and Turkish as the two official languages. Cyprus is classified as a middle-income country, depending mainly on its tourism, which may be regarded as the major economic activity. Also, since 1st of May in 2004, Cyprus has become a full member of the European Union. Furthermore, since January 1, 2008 Cyprus has been a member of the Euro zone, replacing the Cyprus pound with the Euro currency. The island's estimated population is about 1.2 million and the majority of the population is Greek Cypriots. The Ministry of Education, Culture, Youth and Sports is responsible for the implementation of education policy in Cyprus. According to Pashiardis and Tsiakiros (2015) the minister has the highest authority, followed by the permanent secretary. Departments such as the Management, Planning, Registry, and Accounts Office help the overall functioning of the system, which mainly provides education at three main stages: primary, secondary and higher and tertiary which includes public and private universities, as well as public and private colleges or institutes. It is generally accepted that, the Cyprus education system is highly centralized and each school has to follow all the guidelines and directives provided by the Ministry of Education, Culture, Youth and Sports. The Ministry is responsible for the policy making and administrative issues of the governance of education. Also, the Ministry regulates and supervises all the institutions under its jurisdiction and is responsible for the implementation of educational laws and the preparation of new legislation (Pashiardis & Tsiakiros, 2015).

In fact, autonomy is very limited at the school level, as a result of centralization in education governance (Eurydice, 2019). An example of centralization in education is the treatment of Cypriot schools as identical school organizations with identical characteristics and needs, and ignoring the local school culture. In fact, education policy at the school level, which means administering, monitoring and evaluating the quality of education as well as shaping school curriculum, is the responsibility of the Ministry. However, this situation creates a distance from the requirements of the local community and each school organization's culture. In a number of countries, primarily within the so-called Anglo-Saxon world, individual school organizations are considered an important factor for the implementation of local educational policy. On the contrary, in Cyprus there is no such adjustment since educational policy is the responsibility of the Government's Ministerial Council, which sets out school curriculum, textbooks, practices, and different innovations implemented in public schools (Pashiardis, 2004).

On the whole, power within the education system of Cyprus, emanates mainly from the Ministry of Education, Culture, Youth and Sports. Personnel and administrative management, curriculum issues, as well as money allocations are mostly exercised by the Ministry. According to Pashiardis and Tsiakiros (2015), school organizations in Cyprus are financed from state funds based on governmental decisions. Specifically, the state provides the local school boards with funds and then the school boards provide the funds to schools under their jurisdiction. Therefore, most of the decentralized approaches can be found within the school classrooms (Eurydice, 2019). For instance, school teachers in Cyprus enjoy some autonomy in regards to the teaching methods and approaches they use during their teaching process.

Up until now, no major efforts towards decentralization have been noticed. As a consequence, school leaders are obliged to obey without really questioning the system. Despite this situation, the role of school leaders is critical in promoting and sustaining school improvement. In fact, school leaders can act as key factors in shaping their own "internal" educational policy within their school organization and address the specific challenges and needs of the school, based on the local community and the students' socio-economic status. According to Pashiardis and Tsiakiros (2015) a new legislation has been implemented in 2005, where a small amount of money is allocated to each school, and school leaders can use the money as they wish for some extra school expenses (e.g. light equipment etc.) (Eurydice, 2019).

Furthermore, with regards to the accountability process in Cyprus, school organizations do not feel compelled to indicate any form of accountability toward society at large (Pashiardis & Tsiakiros, 2015). In general, a school organization can take an active control in shaping an "internal" educational policy by encouraging the collaboration of the school's internal and external stakeholders. Based on this, the education system in Cyprus needs to move toward more decentralization and empowerment at the school level. However, it is very important to acknowledge that more decentralization and less centralization means responsible and well-prepared school leaders to manage and lead the schools. As a consequence, a more coherent selection and training of the school leaders of the future is a crucial necessity and becomes an imperative (Huber & Pashiardis, 2008).

3 A Decade of Research – The Background of the Study

Many research programs have explored the characteristics of successful school leaders. One of these programs is the International Successful School Principalship Project (ISSPP). The ISSPP program has been actively researching the work of successful school leaders since 2001. Ever since the ISSPP was launched back in 2001, by Prof. Christopher Day in the UK, nobody expected the enormous participation and acceptance of the project's aim and targets. In particular, the ISSPP aimed at the identification of successful school leadership in school organizations of different geographic regions, of different size and with students coming from different social and economic backgrounds (Moos, Krejsle, & Kofod, 2008). To put it simply, taking into account the different changing contexts of school leaders' work, the ISSPP sought to identify similarities as well as dissimilarities in the conditions and work of successful school leaders (Day, 2007). The ISSPP considers itself as a network and not an organization, while each research team in the participating countries seek their own funding. The participation of the first 8 countries (Australia, Canada, China, USA, England, Norway, Sweden, and Denmark) led to the participation, in 2009, of 12 more countries including Cyprus and with additions in 2012 from Spain, Ireland and Chile. To date, 27 countries from the USA, Europe, Africa, Asia and Australia are participating in the ISSPP program. In general, a great number of research cases have been completed which concern the characteristics of successful school leaders (e.g. Day, Parsons, Welsh, & Harris, 2002; Leithwood, Day, Sammons, Harris, & Hopkins, 2006; NCSL, 2006; Day, Leithwood, & Sammons, 2008). Through those pieces of research, the results revealed that successful schools are connected to school leaders' vision and beliefs to transform the school organization through specific actions and practices.

Based on the aforementioned, we present the findings on successful school leadership as they emerged from a research study conducted in Cyprus. Specifically, we synthesize and compare the research results from the primary and secondary education on the island of Cyprus, bringing together the collection of a ten-year research data with regards to successful school leadership. The impetus of this presentation surfaced from two previous papers (Pashiardis et al., 2011, 2012), which referred to the ISSPP research results on the primary and secondary education respectively.

The main purpose of the research activities was to present school leaders' successful characteristics and practices within the context of Cyprus. Also, in order to clarify, we wish to state that the entire ten-year research project was a collective work of two different research teams for primary and secondary education, in which the first author was the principal investigator of both research studies, while the second author participated in the second research team (secondary education).

4   Methods

The collected data were based on an original qualitative empirical research study undertaken through the examination of eleven case studies of successful primary and secondary school leaders. The selection of the schools and school leaders who were included in this piece of research, was based on the recommendations of a team of school inspectors, within the Ministry of Education. Specifically, the selection of the cases was based on school inspectors' acknowledgement that the schools had improved dramatically during the period that these school leaders were in post, no matter how short this period was. A multi-perspective study methodology was followed where data were gathered from a wide range of school stakeholders, such as the school leader, teachers, students and parents employing a common, semi-structured interview protocol for each case (see Day, 2015).

Specifically, the data were collected through interviews based on predetermined research protocols developed through the ISSPP, while the interviews were held with all members of the school organization (school leader, teachers, students, parents). However, in our case the translated (in Greek from English) interview protocols were adjusted to the local context and some questions were modified and others were removed. From our point of you, this process was essential due to the fact that the ISSPP program comes with a variety of methodological approaches, providing more substantial body of knowledge arising from different countries with different contexts through different methodologies. For instance, Bennett (2012) using Furman's ethic of community framework enabled a deeper analysis of democratic processes at a level typically not articulated in other case studies associated with the ISSPP. Also, Møller (2012) in her research combined analyses of public discourses on school leadership with findings based on the ISSPP in order to analyze the school leader's construction of a public face.

In any case, the participation of Cyprus in the ISSPP network provided us with the opportunity to extract valid conclusions and led us to the articulation of certain scientific results, which could then be compared with results on successful school leadership in different countries, different policy and social contexts, both derived from the ISSPP program, as well as other research studies and programs. In this study, we have analyzed and interpreted the results of all case studies, of successful school leaders, and provided a conceptualized presentation of successful school leadership as evidenced within the Cyprus context. Therefore, through content analysis process (constant comparative method), as well as based on the cross-case analysis method both from the results in the primary as well as the secondary education levels, we present the findings from the Cyprus study.

5 The Successful Story from the Cypriot Context – Main Findings

Despite the fact that a school in Cyprus does not have the ability and the freedom to speak up for the implementation of the various educational policies (and in that way school leaders cannot take up new initiatives), successful school leaders do make a difference. In general, school leaders, through the inner and outer inclusion of relevant stakeholders, promote success for the school's mission. At the same time, it seems that particular leadership attributes could, in fact, affect school organizations. Finally, what emerged as an important aspect with regards to successful school leadership in Cyprus was the values aspect. This specific attribute was connected to school leaders' personal values system.

Notably, findings across the Cyprus' school case studies demonstrated that successful school leaders both in primary and secondary education develop external relations, as well as networking with all relevant actors; have a collaborative and shared ownership among their members and within their school organization; and finally promote a clear vision, as well as endorsing a specific number of values. Based on the aforementioned, the following three conceptualized pillars were revealed from the research study in Cyprus: (1) Networked Leadership – Developing external relations, (2) People-centered leadership – Shared ownership and collaborative commitment and (3) Clear vision and values (Figure 5.1). Specifically, in Figure 5.1 the connection of successful attributes, with the three conceptualized pillars are presented. In the following, each pillar is presented thoroughly and in detail. Further information is provided in Section 9.

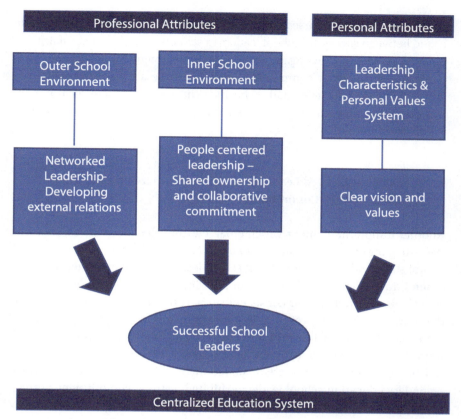

FIGURE 5.1   Successful school leaders' conceptualized pillars in Cyprus

6   Networked Leadership – Developing External Relations

School leaders in primary education exerted an active effort to involve themselves in the community life, which made the locals feel respected by the school leader. On the contrary, in secondary education school leaders gave more attention to the creation of a strong relationship between themselves and the parents' association and parents in general. For example, the (once) deteriorating relationships between parents were fully restored; moreover, school leaders tried to educate parents through lectures and seminars in an effort to gain their support, i.e., in issues such as how to help their children study, what the main characteristics of adolescents are and how can we best deal with them, etc. School leaders also engaged parents in school activities and communicated with the local communities of their schools in order to acquire additional recourses. In general, respect and cooperation were established between successful school leaders in schools and all the external stakeholders, providing once again the important element of networking with parents and the wider community. Specifically, the ability to communicate and collaborate with everybody who may support the school environment was deemed as essential, especially when referring to all the relevant external school stakeholders.

7 People-Centered Leadership – Shared Ownership and Collaborative Commitment

Another important element which emerged from this piece of research was the strong interpersonal relationship between school leaders and the internal school stakeholders. Specifically, all school leaders maintained their visibility around the school, made it a point of showing individual consideration, and actively demonstrated their consistent support for all. Also, school leaders in the primary education proved to be very successful in creating a positive climate, based on mutual respect and cooperation with all stakeholders. Apart from that, secondary education school leaders exhibited democratic characteristics, thus providing a sense of shared ownership into their schools. Also, secondary education school leaders exhibited a strong commitment to their schools, therefore, revealing a transformational leadership style that fosters capacity development and brings higher levels of personal commitment amongst "followers" to organizational objectives. Furthermore, in both situations, an inclusive leadership approach was used in order to increase ownership of the school goals.

8 Clear Vision and Values

Finally, school leaders in both the primary and secondary education sectors constructed a clear vision about the direction their school organization was heading, in relation to the pedagogical aspect of students' academic achievements, as well as with regards to the school's participation in activities and in general concerning the future of the school. Both in primary and secondary education, school leaders have tried to build their vision within their respective school organizations after conducting an internal and external scanning of the school and the local community (Pashiardis, 1996). What was important was the fact that school leaders seemed to develop a clear vision for improving students' learning outcomes and behaviors. In fact, they wanted to communicate this vision to all school stakeholders (both the internal as well as the external). In particular, this school vision was clearly communicated to teachers, students and parents, while school leaders were actively supported by the teachers. With regards to the concept of values, it seems that a particular number of personal values such as the passion, commitment, support and understanding, were actively demonstrated and communicated in order to promote modelling of these expectations by the students and teachers. Even though, this research effort did not proceed to an in-depth investigation of the personal attributes of school leaders, it seems to some extent that this set of values is derived from their personal values system.

9 Discussion of Findings

For Cyprus, as in each country, the educational context is considered an important aspect in order to have successful schools. For instance, the teaching profession in Cyprus remains attractive despite facing specific challenges and has begun to become competitive (European Commission, 2019). However, the action radius of school leadership is limited, since restrictions are still imposed due to the centralized nature of the education system. Nevertheless, this overall presentation of the research study, conducted in Cyprus, led us to the articulation of certain successful practices of school leaders, within a centralized education system, which could be correlated and compared to the results of other successful school leaders in different countries with different educational policies and different social contexts. Also, this effort could build on the collective work of various research projects such as that of the ISSPP (Gurr, 2015). To this end, this holistic presentation of successful school leadership in Cyprus builds upon a substantial body of knowledge emanating from more than 100 case studies across the countries that have been participating in the ISSPP program.

In general, and according to Gurr, Drysdale, Swann, Doherty, Ford, and Goode (2005), school leaders are considered the key of success for a successful school organization. Johnson, Møller, Jacobson, and Wong (2008) stated that school leaders, who participated in the project, took seriously in mind the local context of their school. Specifically, the analysis of various case studies revealed that school leaders choose different practices according to the culture and the local community which their school belongs to. Furthermore, personal characteristics, such as skills and different abilities were crucial for a school leader's success in a school. Apart from that, and to a lesser extent, environmental factors had an influence on successful school leadership (Johnson et al., 2008). Therefore, a thorough discussion of the findings is required, in order to proceed with the perception of school leadership and its enactment in the context of Cyprus.

10 External Leadership Dimension

Firstly, with regards to the professional attributes of successful school leaders in Cyprus, an important finding is connected to the external leadership dimension of school leaders. As it was revealed from the results, successful school leaders in Cyprus seek to create strong relations between themselves and their students' parents, as well as with the local community in general. According to Pashiardis, Pashiardi, and Johansson (2016), across the European continent school leaders create these external alliances by reinforcing, informing and creating relations with the 'outsiders' in order to increase the particular school's success and effectiveness. The important element of alliances by establishing relations not only with the local community but also with the parents underlines the importance of the entrepreneurial leadership style as it was revealed in the Pashiardis and Brauckmann Holistic Leadership Framework (see Pashiardis, 2014; Brauckmann & Pashiardis, 2011). The entrepreneurial leadership style includes the creative utilization of external networks and resources in order to aid the implementation of the school's mission. Gurr (2015) argued that the development of the entrepreneurship leadership approach, by building the capacity of non-teaching staff, is referring mostly to parental involvement, since parents' involvement in schools promotes students' academic development and educational outcomes. He also, mentioned that a key feature of the success of many of the ISSPP school leaders seem to be connected with developing networks, collaborations and partnerships in order to enhance their schools' mission and success.

Current research in Europe demonstrated that school leaders form alliances with other stakeholders outside and around the schools they lead (Brauckmann & Pashiardis, 2016). Specifically, effective school leaders create partnerships with the parents and the wider community of the school, which was also revealed in our current synthesis on successful school leadership. In particular, parents are considered to be an important factor towards school success. This parental involvement, according to Pashiardis (2014), mostly includes the following aspects: (1) parents' involvement in school decision – making; (2) encouragement of a constructive and frequent communication regarding their children's progress and (3) volunteerism in various activities and schools' celebrations. In fact, the above three aspects were observed in the context of Cyprus.

However, what is more interesting is the fact that parental interest in school choice, in conjunction with parental responsibility with regards to their children's learning outcomes, have increased, due to the various reforms in the most developed nations. Some of these reforms include cutting funding, privatization and of course, in some contexts, school decentralization processes, in which schools are allowed more power and autonomy (Yemini, Ramot, & Sagie, 2016). However, this argumentation is mainly associated with parental involvement in a decentralized education environment. On the contrary, in a centralized education system, as in our case, school leaders established relations and collaboration with parents in an effort to support their school through the parents' own professions, to help their children's academic performance, as well as to contribute to the collection of resources and money for various events, etc. due to the limited funding provided by the Ministry. In fact, this was also observed in the Greek context, which has a similar education structure as Cyprus. In a study by Lazaridou and Kassida (2015) the participating school leaders revealed that, due to the limited resources by their Ministry, they were not only in favour of parental participation but also saw a need to increase it.

Furthermore, this external leadership aspect includes also the creation of strategic alliances with other schools and systems, the community, society in general, business and government (Pashiardis, 2014; Brauckmann & Pashiardis, 2011). These overall partnerships may create a safe school environment, encourage the provision of welfare services, improve academic achievement, as well as contribute to the accomplishment of other school goals (Brauckmann, Pashiardis, & Kafa, 2020). In general, within the European context, various pieces of research (e.g. Castro, Expósito-Casas, López-Martín, Lizasoain, Navarro-Asencio, & Gaviria, 2015; Fox & Olsen, 2014; Van Voorhis, Maier, Epstein, & Lloyd, 2013) have revealed that this particular practice is something which (undisputedly) promotes the school's mission and encourages school leaders to achieve their goals, within both a centralized and a decentralized education system. In this respect, successful school leaders can act as entrepreneurs in a variety of ways depending on the level of autonomy and accountability within their respective educational systems (Brauckmann et al., 2020).

Therefore, what can be said is that the external networking could (in fact) support success for a school organization. In particular, the interesting aspect in our case is focused on the fact that, in a centralized educational system this externally oriented leadership dimension (through collaboration and alliances), may be the only way for the school leader to find solutions that arise within the school. In general, the interest to this external leadership aspect is important in today's economic environment.

11 Internal Leadership Dimension

Moving on to another feature of the professional attributes of school leaders, it seems that successful school leaders in Cyprus take into consideration the internal or inner school environment. This particular finding is not something unexpected, since a school leader's work is placed within the school organization along with all the relevant stakeholders, such as teachers and students. Through the findings emerging from the Cyprus study, it seems that successful school leaders involve both the school staff and students towards the creation of the overall school mission. In fact, successful school leaders in Cyprus lead based on strong interpersonal relations, team spirit and by building a positive climate based on mutual cooperation and support. Furthermore, school leaders equally distribute powers and responsibilities to all school staff through a collegial way.

Based on the aforementioned, successful school leaders are enhancing democratic processes within their schools in an effort to be productive. This important finding could be interpreted through the participative leadership style as it was validated in the Pashiardis and Brauckmann Holistic Leadership Framework (see Pashiardis, 2014; Brauckmann & Pashiardis, 2011). This particular leadership style recognizes that school leaders could in fact organize their administrative and management activities through other internal stakeholders, based on their own preferences and the kind of people whom they work with. For instance, Mulford and Silins (2003) argued that effective school leaders promote an administrative and management leadership style through the collaboration of teachers in an effort to promote students' academic achievement. This overall effort could enhance a school's staff commitment to accomplish the school organization's goals as set up in conjunction with the school leader (Leithwood et al., 2006). Based on this finding, successful school leaders could act as transformational leaders who engaged with followers, focused on higher or intrinsic needs, and raise consciousness about the significance of specific outcomes and new ways in which those outcomes might be achieved (Barnett, McCormick, & Conners, 2001; Cox, 2001; Gellis, 2001; Judge & Piccolo, 2004). In a recent study, on low performing schools in Cyprus and the role of school leadership, Pashiardis et al. (2018b) argued that school leaders have created a strong cooperation among the internal school stakeholders, as well as built a healthy relationship and created a respectful surrounding environment. Furthermore, Brauckmann and Pashiardis (2016) supported that successful school leaders around Europe create, sustain and nurture teams within their school organization in an effort to provide solutions. Therefore, what could be said is the fact that successful school leaders take into consideration the internal aspect of their school organizations in order to build internal stability.

12   Personal Attributes Leadership Dimension

Finally, with regards to the personal attributes of successful school leadership in Cyprus, school leaders constructed a structured vision with regards to the school organization's future about students' learning outcomes. According, to other studies on successful school leadership, conducted in various contexts (e.g. Giles, Jacobson, Johnson, & Ylimaki, 2007; Leithwood & Riehk, 2003), successful school leaders redesigned their school organization in order to improve performance and at the same time they shared their vision with the school staff. In fact, in a recent study in Cyprus (Pashiardis et al., 2018b), school leaders in low performing schools had a vision, which was oriented in restructuring the school organization. In order to do that, school leaders perceived external forces as an opportunity to spread their new vision (Pashiardis et al., 2018b). Therefore, we could argue that both personal and professional attributes could in fact be intertwined. Specifically, by taking into consideration the blending of the various internal and external stakeholders in order to fulfil their vision.

At the same time, successful school leaders promoted a number of particular personal values such as that of commitment, support and understanding which are based on their own personal values system. Veritably, much of the literature (e.g. Gold, 2004; Baig, 2010; Notman, 2014; Crow & Møller, 2017; Kafa & Pashiardis, 2019) suggests that school leadership is values – driven and claims that personal values act as an influential variable in a school leader's actions, such as the way they articulate their relationships with students and teachers, as well as their school's aspirations and expectations. In a study by Kafa and Pashiardis (2019), on school leaders' personal values systems in Cyprus, a school principal, in his effort to build relationships and contacts with various external stakeholders such as parents etc., promoted a number of values such as kindness and commitment.

Based on the aforementioned, as can be seen in Figure 5.2, successful school leadership in Cyprus is structured through the combination of particular professional and personal attributes that affect and/or interact with the internal and external dimensions of a school organization. Consequently, it could be stressed that successful school leaders in Cyprus, within its centralized education system, could in fact create and promote an "internal" educational policy leading toward the success of the school through a combination of particular professional and personal attributes that include the participation of internal and external school stakeholders.

Under the light of this ascertainment, school leadership is highly contextualized not only at the system level, but also (and particularly) at the school level and it can be formed through the sum of both professional and personal

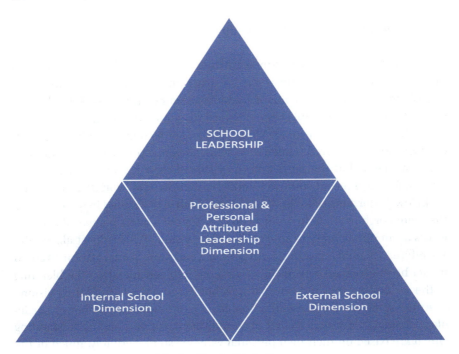

FIGURE 5.2   Practicing successful school leadership in Cyprus

attributes which school leaders, as human beings, posses. This interaction between the professional and the personal perspective provide equal attention to both the internal and the external school aspect.

13   Conclusions and Implications

In this study, we have presented the overall research results on successful school leaders in the Cypriot context. Drawing upon the findings of this exploration we argue that successful school leaders are those who combined successful practices both within the internal and external environment of the school organization. The aforementioned presentation of the summary findings contributes to the better understanding and capture of the successful characteristics and practices of successful school leaders in the Cypriot context and can be compared with other research studies on successful school leadership in other contexts, both in centralized and decentralized education systems. In general, there is no doubt that high caliber successful school leaders are considered especially important for the organization and functioning of successful schools.

However, the sense-making of successful school leadership must be seen in relation to the context in which people are located and the values underpinning the school as an institution in society (Dimmock & Walker, 2000). In fact, the concept of school leadership is a mixture of various school practices (Brauckmann & Pashiardis, 2008), guided by professional and personal attributes. What is more interesting is the fact that the attention nowadays is shifted to the (relatively) new management system philosophy called New Public Management (NPM), as a policy response to various educational, societal and economic changes (Brauckmann, Pashiardis, & Kafa, 2020) occurring in the European context. This NPM approach is characterized by greater degrees of Autonomy, Accountability, School voice and Choice.

Recently, Brauckmann, Pashiardis, and Ärlestig (2020) argued that since context and school leadership actions are intertwined, school leadership preparation programs must adopt some of those policies guided by the concept of NPM. This is considered important since these NPM approaches are aiming to make school organizations more effective, efficient, evidence-oriented and successful (Brauckmann et al., 2020). At the same time, caution should be exercised, since the three pillars of NPM will not always lead to school improvement; on the contrary, there is ample research which tells us that too much autonomy, accountability and parental choice may result in producing more inequalities within the various education systems (Hanushek, 2019; Hanushek, Link, & Woessmann, 2013; Woessmann, 2003).

Furthermore, Schwarz and Brauckmann (2015) argued that the area close to school (ACTS) acts as an intermediate context level of school leadership. Both researchers, argued that limited research has been conducted with regards to the role of the area close to school as a moderator between structural characteristics (notably student composition) and school leadership actions. Therefore, it is important to take into consideration, the relationship of the successful practices of school leaders in conjunction with the area and the environment that constitutes their immediate context.

As a consequence, the training of school leaders and specifically leadership preparation programs, need to be context-sensitive and provide stronger consideration of contextual factors including the national and local areas (Brauckmann et al., 2020). Additionally, it is very important to provide this kind of preparation programs in a more inclusive way, which includes both theory and practice. For example, these particular successful school leadership practices in a centralized educational system as emerged from the Cyprus study could form the basis for training programs of other countries in the EU with a similar background of the education system and culture.

Finally, it is worth noting that the ISSPP recently presented the new revised interview protocols on successful school leadership. Based on the interview protocols that have been used in this research study, the ISSPP introduced the revised protocols in order for country members to conduct new and updated research on successful school leadership within their contexts. Then, participating countries will conduct research and highlight successful school leaders' characteristics and practices of the next decade, whilst they will provide a comparative approach of the research results conducted within their context a decade ago (for a more recent dialogue on successful and effective school leaders and schools, please see Pashiardis & Johansson, 2020).

As a final thought, the impact of the research and study, both during the previous decade and the anticipated new results about school leadership could in fact further advance the practice of successful school leadership by enhancing the existing theoretical and conceptual knowledge in various educational contexts around the world.

References

Baig, S. (2010). The place of personal values in educational leadership in Pakistan. *Values and Ethics in Educational Administration, 8*(3), 1–8.

Barnett, K., McCormick, J., & Conners, R. (2001). Transformational leadership in schools – Panacea, placebo or problem? *Journal of Educational Administration, 39*(1), 24–46.

Bennett, J. (2012). "Democratic" collaboration for school turnaround in Southern Arizona. *International Journal of Educational Management, 26*(5), 442–451.

Brauckmann, S., & Pashiardis P. (2008). New educational governance and educational leadership: Investigating the foundations of a new relationship. In *Conference Proceedings of the Greek Pedagogical Institute* (pp. 199–233). Greek Pedagogical Institute.

Brauckmann, S., & Pashiardis, P. (2011). A validation study of the leadership styles of a holistic leadership theoretical framework. *International Journal of Educational Management, 25*(2), 11–32.

Brauckmann, S., & Pashiardis, P. (2016). European perspectives. In P. Pashiardis & O. Johansson (Eds.), *Successful school leadership. International perspectives* (pp. 179–191). Bloomsbury.

Brauckmann, S., Pashiardis, P., & Ärlestig, H. (2020). Bringing context and educational leadership together: Fostering the professional development of school principals. *Professional Development in Education*. doi:10.1080/19415257.2020.1747105

Brauckmann, S., Pashiardis, P., & Kafa, A. (2020). Leadership approaches and practices under the paradigm of new public management – An entrepreneurial perspective on parental involvement. *IPRASE Journal*. doi:10.32076/RA11107

Castro, M., Expósito-Casas, E., López-Martín, E., Lizasoain, L., Navarro-Asencio, E., & Gaviria, J. L. (2015). Parental involvement on student academic achievement: A meta-analysis. *Educational Research Review, 14*, 33–46.

Cox, P. L. (2001). Transformational leadership: A success story at Cornell University. In *Proceedings of the ATEM/AAPPA 2001 conference*. http://www.anu.edu.au/facilities/atem-aappaa/full_papers/Coxkeynote.html

Crow, G., & Møller, J. (2017). Professional identities of school leaders across international contexts: An introduction and rationale. *Educational Management Administration & Leadership, 45*(3), 1–10.

Day, C. (2007). What being a successful principal really means: An international perspective. *Educational Leadership and Administration: Teaching and Program Development, 19*, 13–24.

Day C., Gu, Q., & Sammons, P. (2016). The impact of leadership on student outcomes: How successful school leaders use transformational and instructional strategies to make a difference. *Educational Administration Quarterly, 52*(2), 221–258.

Day, C., & Leithwood, K. (2007). *Successful school principalship in times of change: An international perspective.* Springer.

Day, C., Leithwood, K., & Sammons, P. (2008). What we have learned, what we need to know more about. *School Leadership & Management, 28*(1), 83–96.

Day, C., Parsons, C., Welsh, P., & Harris, A. (2002). Improving leadership: Room for improvement? *Improving Schools, 5*(1), 36–51.

Dimmock, C., & Walker, A. (2000). Cross-cultural values and leadership. *Management in Education, 14*(3), 21–24.

Elmore, R. (2000). *Building a new structure for school leadership.* Albert Shanker Institute.

European Commission. (2019). *Education and training monitor 2019 – Cyprus.* Publications Office of the European Union. https://ec.europa.eu/education/sites/education/files/document-library-docs/et-monitor-report-2019-cyprus_en.pdf

Eurydice. (2019). *Key features of the education system: Cyprus.* https://eacea.ec.europa.eu/national-policies/eurydice/content/cyprus_en

Fox, S., & Olsen, A. (2014). *Education capital: Our evidence base. Defining parental engagement.* Australian Research Alliance for Children and Youth.

Fullan, M. (2001). *The new meaning of educational change* (3rd ed.). Routledge-Falmer Publications.

Gellis, Z. D. (2001). Social work perceptions of transformational and transactional leadership in health care. *Social Work Research, 25*(1), 17–25.

Giles, C., Jacobson, S., Johnson, L., & Ylimaki, R. (2007). Against the odds: Successful principals in challenging U.S. schools. In C. Day & K. Leithwood (Eds.), *Successful principal leadership in times of change* (pp. 155–169). Springer.

Gold, A. (2004). *Values and leadership.* Institute of Education, University of London.

Gurr, D. (2015). A model of successful school leadership from the international successful school principalship project. *Societies, 5*, 136–150.

Gurr, D., Drysdale, L., Longmuir, F., & McCrohan, K. (2018). Leading the improvement of schools in challenging circumstances. *International Studies in Educational Administration, 46*(1), 22–44.

Gurr, D., Drysdale, L., Swann, R., Doherty, J., Ford, P., & Goode, H. (2005). *The International Successful School Principalship Project (ISSPP): Comparison across country case studies*. Paper presented at the Australian Council for Educational Leaders National Conference, Gold Coast.

Hanushek, E. A. (2019). Education and the growth: Equity trade-off. In C. Hulten & V. Ramey (Eds.), *Education, skills and technical change: Implications for future U.S. GDP growth* (pp. 293–312). University of Chicago Press.

Hanushek, E. A., Link, S., & Woessmann, L. (2013). Does school autonomy make sense every-where? Panel estimates from PISA. *Journal of Development Economics, 104,* 212–232.

Huber, S., & Pashiardis, P. (2008). The recruitment and selection of school leaders. In G. Crow, J. Lumby, & P. Pashiardis (Eds.), *International handbook on the preparation and development of school leaders* (pp. 176–220). Routledge.

Jacobson, S., & Day, C. (2007). The International Successful School Principalship Project (ISSPP): An overview of the project, the case studies and their contexts. *International Studies in Educational Administration, 35*(3), 3–10.

Jacobson, S., Johnson, L., Ylimaki, R., & Giles, C. (2005). Successful leadership in challenging U.S. schools: Enabling principles, enabling schools. *Journal of Educational Administration, 43*(6), 607–618.

Johnson, L., Møller, J., Jacobson, S., & Wong, K. (2008). Cross-national Comparisons in the International Successful School Principalship Project (ISSPP): The USA, Norway and China. *Scandinavian Journal of Educational Research, 52*(4), 407–422.

Judge, T. A., & Piccolo, R. F. (2004). Transformational and transactional leadership: A meta-analytic test of their relative validity. *Journal of Applied Psychology, 89*(5), 755–768.

Kafa, A., & Pashiardis, P. (2019). Exploring school principals' personal identities in Cyprus from a values perspective. *International Journal of Educational Management, 33*(5), 886–902.

Lazaridou, A., & Kassida, A. G. (2015). Involving parents in secondary schools: Principals' perspectives in Greece. *International Journal of Educational Management, 29*(1), 98–114.

Leithwood, K., Day, C., Sammons, P., Harris, A., & Hopkins, D. (2006). *Successful school leadership: What it is and how it influences pupil learning* (Research, No. RR800). National College for School Leadership.

Leithwood, K., & Riehl, C. (2003). *What do we already know about successful school leadership?* Paper presented at the Annual Meeting of the American Educational Research Association, Chicago, IL.

McLaughlin, M., & Talbert, J. (2001). *Professional communities and the work of high school teaching*. University of Chicago Press.

Møller, J. (2012). The construction of a public face as a school principal. *International Journal of Educational Management, 26*(5) 452–460.

Moos, L., Krejsler, J., & Kofod, K. (2008). Successful principals: Telling or selling? On the important of context for school leadership. *International Journal of Leadership in Education, 11*(4), 341–352.

Mulford, B., & Silins, H. (2003). Leadership for organizational learning and improved student outcomes – What do we know? *Cambridge Journal of Education, 33*(2), 175–195.

National College for School Leadership. (2006). *What we know about school leadership*. Author.

Newmann, F. M., King, B., & Youngs, P. (2000). Professional development that addresses school capacity: Lessons from urban elementary schools. *American Journal of Education, 108*(4), 259–299.

Nielson, B. (2008). *Difference between leadership and management.* http://ezinearticles.com/index.php?Difference-Between-Leadership/

Notman, R. (2017). Professional identity, adaptation and the self: Cases of New Zealand school principals during a time of change. *Educational Management Administration & Leadership, 45*(5), 1–15.

Pashiardis, P. (1996). Environmental scanning in educational organizations: Uses, approaches, sources and methodologies. *International Journal of Educational Management, 10*(3), 5–9.

Pashiardis, P. (Ed.). (2014). *Modeling school leadership across Europe: In search of new frontiers*. Springer.

Pashiardis, P., & Brauckmann, S. (2009). The leadership cocktail. In *The leadership cocktail, A highly contextual mix*. LISA.

Pashiardis, P., Brauckmann, S., & Kafa, A. (2018a). Leading low performing schools in Cyprus: Finding pathways through internal and external challenges. *Leading and Managing, 24*(2), 14–27.

Pashiardis, P., Brauckmann, S., & Kafa, A. (2018b). Let the context become your ally: School Principalship in two cases from low performing schools in Cyprus. *School Leadership & Management.* doi:10.1080/13632434.2018.1433652

Pashiardis, P., & Johansson, O. (2016). What is successful and effective school leadership? In P. Pashiardis & O. Johansson (Eds.), *Successful school leadership. International perspectives* (pp. 1–12). Bloomsbury.

Pashiardis, P., & Johansson, O. (2020). Successful and effective schools: Bridging the gap. *Educational Management, Administration and Leadership.* doi:10.1177/1741143220932585

Pashiardis, P., Kafa, A., & Marmara, C. (2012). A case study of successful secondary principalship in Cyprus: What have 'Thucydides' and 'Plato' revealed to us? *International Journal of Educational Management, 26*(5), 480–493.

Pashiardis, P., Pashiardi, G., & Johansson, O. (2016). Understanding the impact of successful and effective school leadership as practiced. In P. Pashiardis & O. Johansson (Eds.), *Successful school leadership. International perspectives* (pp. 195–207). Bloomsbury.

Pashiardis, P., Savvides, V., Lytra, E., & Angelidou, K. (2011). Successful school leadership in rural contexts: The case of Cyprus. *Educational Management, Administration and Leadership, 39*(5), 536–553.

Pashiardis, P., & Tsiakiros, A. (2015). Cyprus. In W. Hörner, H. Döbert, L. Reuter, & B. von Kopp (Eds.), *The education systems of Europe* (pp. 173–186). Global Education Systems/Springer.

Schwarz, A., & Brauckmann, S. (2015). *Between facts and perceptions: The area close to school as a context factor in school leadership* (Schumpeter Discussion Papers SDP15003). Schumpeter School of Business and Economics, University of Wuppertal.

Van Voorhis, F. L., Maier, M. F., Epstein, J. L., & Lloyd, C. M. (2013). *The impact of family involvement on the education of children ages 3 to 8: A focus on literacy and math achievement outcomes and social-emotional skills.* http://www.mdrc.org/sites/default/files/The_Impact_of_Family_Involvement_FR.pdf

Wang, L. H., Gurr, D., & Drysdale, L. (2016). Successful school leadership: Case studies of four Singapore primary schools. *Journal of Educational Administration, 54*(3), 270–287.

Woessmann, L. (2003). Schooling resources, educational institutions, and student performance: The international evidence. *Oxford Bulletin of Economics & Statistics, 65*(2), 117–170.

Yemini, M., Ramot, R., & Sagie, N. (2016). Parental 'intrapreneurship' in action: Theoretical elaboration through the Israeli case study. *Educational Review, 68*(2), 239–255.

CHAPTER 6

Educational Leadership in Algeria: A Decisive Factor in the 2004 Higher Education Reform

Mohamed Miliani

Abstract

The present chapter considers leadership as an essential invariant of the micropolitics of universities and a strong adverse-impact parameter on the last reform that was launched in 2004 in the Algerian universities. Socially speaking, educational leadership fascinates first because of material advantages supposedly attached to it. Internally, at university level, and despite the various forms and patterns of power, the reform of higher education has showed shortcomings and malfunctions that could be attributed to weak or lack of leadership. The first university evaluations (mid-term assessment in 2006, audits in 2010, and external evaluations in 2011) have stressed that the reform had suffered from drawbacks in the pedagogy used, the determination of curricula and minimal teacher training. However, leaders of the administration, namely the rectors, deans and department-heads, have always been publicly spared from criticism by the '*Tutelle*' (line ministry).

In the present reflection, the focus will be on the roles of these university leaders who exercise organizational authority towards the implementation of the '*Licence-Master-Doctorat*' (LMD) reform. Our presumption is that even if educational leadership is not attributable to these appointed or co-opted leaders, their own liability is not negligible though their accountability is never mentioned.

Educational leadership, understood as the performativity and positional authority of these university officials, is exercised daily on other stakeholders, in the form of follow-up, counselling, monitoring and evaluation of practices and tasks. An analysis was necessary to evaluate the role of educational leadership as seen by a number of stakeholders through unstructured interviews. Another corpus was central to understanding internal relations, namely the Algerian university ethics and deontology charter elaborated in 2010 by the Ministry of Higher Education.

A global assessment of the achievements of the 2004 reform showed that the changes that were supposed to occur were far from being concretely achieved in the field. This has been confirmed by the universities' self-evaluations in 2018. Is it then a problem of the internal dynamics (dominance, control and/or resistance from one or several actors)? On the other hand, are the leaders' limited capabilities or inappropriate leadership styles at the origin of the little effectiveness and efficiency of the reform where responsibility (organizational and academic) has been considered the less significant variable of all? It appears that the mission of the leaders is so restricted that it only approximates that of a caretaker (of students, staff and university structures), while supervising, for the most part, the yearly increasing university cohorts.

Keywords

leadership – reform – higher education – university ethics and deontology charter

1 Introduction

In the early 2000s, a major education reform surge took place in Algeria, under the strong pressure of the government targeting the whole education system. Two simultaneous reforms took place, the covert one in 2003 at school level under the aegis of the Ministry of National Education (MNE). the other one, in 2004, more publicized, though said to be slow and progressive, was introduced at higher level (Ministry of Higher Education and Scientific Research, MoHE) to bring about a new scheme labelled LMD[1] ('licence/BA, Master and doctorate' inspired by the Bologna Process) in universities, generating overnight antagonistic feelings and reactions. The main reason for this is that any reform triggers off politically biased reactions more or less subtle or open against those who have authority and/or power. The LMD reform did meet oppositions of various nature and scope. This is why, between 2004 and 2011, when MoHE decided to generalize the system in all university entities of the country, the authorities had all the difficulties in the world to implement the aforementioned reform. What was often said to be the core problem was the content and structuration of the reform leaving aside the criticism expressed against the institutional authorities' leadership out of sheer opposition or because of conflicting political agendas. The main reason was that the university communities were not agreed on which change was needed most and whether the intended change was expected or even wanted. In fact, the leaders' supposed methods and actions gathered the bulk of criticism from all sides that are the core of this investigation. Is this due to internal dynamics, or the leaders' background, academic rank or management styles, or rather the limited effectiveness and efficiency of their policies and managerial practices after more than fifteen years of implementation of the reform?

Having been involved in the implementation of the reform in the faculties of foreign languages, one saw differing attitudes and motivations that did not augur well for the reform. Various justifications have been put forward as an explanation of people's refusal to participate in the reform actions or more their rejection of it. Not many mentioned the educational leadership at the meso (rectors and directors of universities) and micro levels (deans and heads of faculties) as a potential factor of malfunction. Our intention here is to analyse the dysfunctions of the reform we believe to be due to a great extent to leadership or rather the lack of it in the management of the reform. One has tried to evaluate how much this factor has reduced the chances of success of the reform. Some might even say that the reform is a total failure due to a network of parameters adversely affecting the outcomes of the reform. As an explanation, one hypothesises that educational leadership, which is not just the responsibility (Author, 2016) of those who are very often co-opted leaders, is in many ways the weakest link in the Algerian context. Our reflection will refer to official documents of different sorts (ministerial notes, decrees, circulars, etc.), and a corpus constituted by the views and experiences of staff[2] in academic and scientific positions ranging from rectors, vice-rectors, deans and department heads. With these semi-structured interviews[3], we have tried to understand and evaluate the part played by these leaders in the implementation of the reform. Likewise, we thought it useful to use, when necessary, press articles to gauge the external voices' evaluation of this matter. The press has never stopped reporting the many counterproductive reactions to the reform from those concerned but also of analysts from different backgrounds and lifestyles. Ultimately, we wish to problematize the internal dynamics of the university institution, mainly its capacity to evolve and innovate, or not, and the leaders' herculean tasks to impose or not their style of leadership when given exceptional tasks like managing the university reform with little means and leeway. In the present reflection, one will try to unveil the intricacies of university leadership in Algeria and its impact on their commitment and efficiency of organizational performance when implementing the reform that took years (from 2004 to 2010) before all HE institutions were forced to adopt the LMD scheme. Our argument draws from the notion of micropolitics in order to understand why leadership, embodied in a number of persons, was not as decisive as was expected by all stakeholders but principally by the reform initiator, the government. Consequently, many people, namely teachers and students, blamed the university decision-makers for the failure of the process that ended with a reform that was finished by 'amendments, changes and complementation' (Benghebrit et al., 2009, p. 193). Said bluntly, the reform seemed patchy to many education experts.

2   The University as Educational Organization

There are about one hundred and six HE establishments[4] in the whole system managed by MoHE. The student population is around 1,700,000. If one adds this to the number of pupils in national education, around 9 million, this approximates the population of Tunisia (11,775,621). This huge population has compelled the State to invest heavily in education. Its budget is second after that of the army. In higher education, the shift of paradigm from a policy of means, from the 1960s to the mid-2010s, to one of results, in the last five years, has failed to change an institution that is still lagging behind worldwide. In fact, the universities are having problems adjusting to the new idea of their own future within the logic of a market economy while aiming at students' employability. The latter is a concept that is hard to understand by people who are accustomed to the idea of a never-ending sustained state-help, but in keeping with the principle of the rent to be distributed to all. As a learning organization, the Algerian university is experiencing a real revolution of mentalities when confronted with the outside world where international university rankings are dominating debates and narratives. The other taboo issue concerns the continuing and systematic avoidance of financing and non-gratuitous studies the State ignores superbly. More, team-learning, collaborative pedagogies with critical thinking seem to belong to a world of make-believe, which does not go with the prevailing culture. The LMD reform is certainly not just about new curricula and tutoring. This is a fact that has barely caused a ripple from the decision-takers.

It is the 03-279 executive decree of August 23 that fixed the missions, tasks and rules for the organization and functioning of the university (Official Bulletin of the Algerian Republic No 5124 of August 24th, 2003). Its Article 25 determines for universities the composition of the Rectorate around the rector (comprising the governing board: vice-rectors, secretary general, deans and the library curator). Further, article 27 stipulates, 'the rector is responsible for the general functioning of the university in respect for the prerogatives of its other bodies'. The other roles bestowed on him are basic: he represents the university, exercises authority, concludes contracts, monitors the application of legislation and current regulation, delegates power of signature, nominates personnel, ensures respect for the rules of procedures, and maintains law, discipline and order and finally awards diplomas by delegation. Nothing is thus particularly creative in these tasks and actions where leadership serves no purpose. In fact, the Ministry is totally focussed on the refoundation of a sector that is still given the main, if not the sole mission, of absorbing the large cohorts of baccalaureate-holders, hoping in the long run to best meet the needs of the productive sector that is trying to survive on its own. However, this sounds like a repetitive incantation in an economic environment that is plagued by the informal market evaluated at 40% of the economy. Thus, wishful thinking and sloganeering substitute long-term visions. In the questionnaire given to twelve (12) executives to get their own description of their position as leaders, no respondent chose the option: visionary, when asked to suggest a salient characteristic of university leaders. The fact is that the university is considered as a political system consisting, among other things, of cooperative and conflictive parameters that end up with alliances, coalitions, partnerships, obligations, duties and responsibilities. Hence, no two situations faced by these leaders are identical. To analyse these processes, our angle of investigation focuses on micropolitics, i.e., the use of formal and informal power by the community of practice, whether by individuals or interest groups, to achieve their intended objectives that may not be common or even shared. This approach to the analysis of educational leadership may permit to delve into the perceptions and attitudes behind the actions of those involved in the reform. In particular, those invested with the power to bring change to a system that has shown dysfunctions, but who find themselves facing interlocutors with different visions and interests, the very causes of conflicts, disengagement and/or struggles.

Despite the fact that the university is a relatively traditional institution, in the sense that it has been busy since independence, maintaining the status quo, the last two years have seen another top-down ministerial injunction to incite universities to draw up individual development projects for 2021. The aim was to pressure the university establishments to start modernizing their governance, their Achilles' heel, thus making their moves in opposite directions between centralization and autonomy. Indeed, the key notion of autonomy, often talked about and associated with (radical) change, is rarely visible in the field. It is also true that universities are torn between their concern for the management of student flux they receive year in year out without any stringent criterion for selection and the needs of an environment that does not trust universities. As an educational organization, the average Algerian university is also juggling with, on the one hand, scarce means and resources, and on the other more and more restless, demanding critical student associations[5]. The educational authorities are thus trying to take up this challenge while providing students with generous benefits for self-financing purposes, inside or outside university.

3   HE Reform: A Disarming Top-Down Process

The 2004 reform started progressively, first with only ten pilot universities, before it was generalized to all fifty universities in 2011. The whole reform package could not be delivered from the start, hence the primary focus on curricula development in certain study domains[6] and specialities. From 2002, a preparatory phase started to renew all curricula involving high-level professors to elaborate 'architectures' of the 'licence' (BA) degree in an urgency that added more difficulties and complexity to the mission. Paradoxically, nearly all university leaders were brushed aside from the process, which at the end deepened their ignorance of the reform components (pedagogy and governance). Its implementation has been top-down from start to finish, which is a way to quicken things up, following the ministry's agenda, and conversely, avoiding opposition or resistance. However, the ministry was far from the realities of the field:

> ... reality of the institutions whose functioning is not only determined by the principle of uniformity of funding, uniformity and pedagogical levelling, but also by a heavy dependence on centralized guidelines, given that little initiative, skills and freedom are left to the discretion of rulers through permanent and tight reports to the 'Tutelle'. (Zaid, 2018, p. 18)

The university leaders acted administratively, a job they had not been trained in. The ultimate paradox was that the Ministry had pledged to follow a supposedly cooperative and consensual process while avoiding gathering teachers around the project of reforming a system that had been rejected by a majority. A large proportion of stakeholders declared the undertaking potentially conflictive and adverse to their own vision, because many declared that they had not been involved, worse, they had been marginalized. In fact, the second act, namely the implementation itself, was left to university officials (deans and department heads) who were neither fully informed nor trained, but had to deal with opposition from the start. This spelt more difficulties and strikes from teachers and students who rebuffed the reform. It is therefore very unlikely for a leader to play an active role[7] when opposition is rough and the ministerial injunctions highly pressing. At times, the leaders had to negotiate, against their own will, from a weak position due to their lack of understanding of the ins and outs of the reform, perhaps also their lack of engagement.

On the other hand, the press[8] targeted the reform as being unworkable and unrealistic without proper financial, human and technological means. The intensity of the pressures was such that the rectors had to face criticism from different partners while pursuing their journey, which route had not been defined clearly from the start. The fact that the reform was progressive helped each pedagogical entity to choose the time and importance of the training offers to provide to fresher. Despite this, the reform was advancing willy-nilly because of the incompleteness of its package (methodology, evaluation, tutoring came later). This sentiment of uncertainty and unfinished business, played against the pretention of several university decision-makers to lead the way[9] with a reform that was incomplete. On the contrary, on the field, responsibility followed a 'cascade' effect: each official passing to their subordinates the responsibility to do, decide and deliver, at times with no referring text, ministerial note or else.

4 The Micropolitics of Leadership in HE

At the heart of the reform lies the micropolitics of educational change and stability of the institution, something humans are condemned to endure. Their organizational life is subjected to forces that promote or pursue innovation and change, which creates tensions among any given community of practice that should learn to live with these. Indeed, "the micropolitical relationships within the university unveils what is at stake between two seemingly unrelated spheres (the political and the educational): the management of the oil rent" (Author, 2003, p. 63). Nevertheless, questions like: 'Who pilots the university change? Who selects the decision-making processes? What is the degree of autonomy universities enjoy[10]? Who takes the initiatives to do and be decisive?' remain unanswered because of lack of visibility of the chain decision. In fact, the ordering body was anything but the official leader because the university is a hierarchical organizational structure where formal and informal hierarchy mix, and where covert and overt powers coexist. Such an organization is too rigid but could go on with the kind of leaders the officials are. However, that does not explain why real power is within the hands of the administrative officials[11]. The interview with the group of leaders has partially answered these concerns by selecting the style of leadership they thought they exercised or observed around them. The most practised was the bureaucratic style (5) geared towards rules and procedures, the second choice was the autocratic leader (1) looking for results at any cost, followed by the incentive-driven transactional style (4) and finally, the democratic (2) interested in teamwork. There was no surprise when no one suggested the visionary who could inspire, or the performance-oriented pacesetter. None chose the laissez-faire or the hands-off leadership styles, which in itself is rather comforting! However, their nomination has not changed over decades of practice, for there is a problem of governance:

> Indeed, the democratization of higher education that benefited millions of Algerians has not been accompanied by democratization of its man-

agement. Rectors, and other directors of academic institutions, continue to be appointed by ministerial orders without the entire University community' voice in this regard. Designations are much more responsive to considerations of political nature than criteria of competence or scientific authority. Despite many protest movements initiated by teachers, the Ministry has always opposed outright refusal to this claim of democratization. For this one, it is otherwise easier to manage administrators appointed by him than to have to deal with officials democratically elected by their peers. (Bessadi, 2017)

At university level, decisions seem to pertain to two unrelated spheres (pedagogy and administration) despite their close nature and their convergence under the aegis of the leader(s). Nevertheless, the administrative side has, contrary to common sense, the upper hand over pedagogy and science, surely, remnants from the colonial system used to Jacobin administrative traditions. Who speaks to whom? For which purpose? About which matter? Briefly, who dictates the way matters are raised, dealt with and solved (like implementing a reform)? Which hierarchy is legitimate? What is the result of routine and bad practice? Overall, decision-making processes are the less talked about matter, even if content of decisions benefits all university stakeholders. Are there not conflicts of authority? Are the leaders conscious of them? How do they solve them? Who gives orders? Who is supposed to do the follow-up? Who is accountable for the outcomes obtained, be it success or failure? We hypothesize that though educational leadership was supposed to play a decisive part in the implementation of the 2004 HE reform, things did not go as expected. However, what is less clear is the definition of what leadership means within a complex setting where the parameters are of a political (one party-state for a long time), cultural (favouring cultural monolithism), and even religious nature (where submission is the required attitude of believers). However, from the interviews, one could make out that leadership is lived as a day-to-day challenge that calls for basic pragmatism, intuition and constant care because of lack of collective vision of the undertaking: it is more of a solitary process. The leader never knows what tomorrow can hold for him, when he might be disqualified and forced to quit, with no explanation from those in power! Power[12] is a constant thorny issue in universities, one could split into cooperative, consensual, conflictive and coercive. This typology adds more difficulty to understand the multidimensional ways university leaders function and behave. It also underlines the complexity of the 'leading people' task in an organizational entity where things do not always go as planned and where the time factor is an elastic datum.

The reform suffered from a number of hindrances and hitches: resistance on the part of teachers who feared politicking from the authorities; panic of students about the new system; and disagreement of parents who were not in favour of something that seemed to devalue the old training scheme (studies duration reduced from 4 to 3 years). Pedagogically speaking, innovation was not on the teachers' agenda while the reform asked them to renew their curricula to adapt them to the exigencies of the market, something the leaders could not control, confining themselves simply to determining the division of labour between partners. This is why leaders sought a variety of strategies to organize their professional lives: "… by which individuals and groups in organizational context seek to use their resources of power and influence to further their interests" (Hoyle, 1982, p. 88). These strategies display a wide range of choices between extreme authoritarianism and complete laissez-faire. Besides, and despite the university staff demand for more autonomy of management, MoHE exerted its power in a subtle way, using committees and commissions to distribute orders thus avoiding confrontations with key partners who saw reform imposition as politicking in its finest display. On the other hand, students' associations[13] started to negotiate their own existence with peace in the campuses. The role of the institutional leaders was shrinking fast which did not help them much to intervene in conflicts, even if the intention was to bring together all partners to cooperate with one another. The main challenge of the leaders was to find the most adequate responses[14] to the centrality of decisions as imposed by the ministry far from field realities. The administrative straitjacket devised by the ministry consisted of a number of entities, committees[15] and bodies that ended up minimizing the work of leaders to mere reporting of the execution of orders in a way to manage the status quo. One of the recurrent remarks made by the questioned was that they felt more like administrators not managers.

5 The University Leaders: between Loyalty, Compromise and Routine

One key issue towards the understanding of the educational leadership's role in the reform can be put in the form of a rather complex question: "How do leaders think and act?" within a context, that is crushing and infantilizing people through top-down procedures. Along the same vein, Schön (1983) has provided a useful operational question: 'How do professionals think in action?' The educational leaders think and act daily, but have these decision-makers weighed all their options through a logical process of deliberation, while or before acting? A study by Hirschman (1970) helped us encompass all the complexity of decision taking within work relations where the individuals can either exit (leave a relationship), voice (express their inner thoughts, or even protest) or stay loyal because they are considered as agents of implantation (Duclos, 2015) through the injunction of the ministry. However, both the institution and the leader understand this as duty. Indeed, in such a situation, the leader is simply following the code of deontological ethics geared towards conformity to duty,[16] even if leaders develop an intuitive code that sets the norms of conduct in the workplace. It is true that the existing code of university ethics and deontology (2010, CUED) is unknown to a majority of stakeholders who could refer to it. The code states clearly that: "the main responsibility of the teacher-researcher is to fully warrant its academic functions". In this case, responsibility, understood as duty or even submission and obedience, seems to iron out the potential conflicts between the leaders and their colleagues. The teacher-researcher must 'try to comply with the norms as high as possible in his professional activity' (CUED). Indeed, common benefit imposes to the leader to act 'professionally', while helping with the implementation of the reform to the best of his knowledge. At times, it is only a personal engagement to fight against those who manifest an adverse attitude to the reform. The 'executor' acts according to his own principles that push him to act as a responsible person whose power is nevertheless institutional (Bourdieu & Passeron, 1970). He is then forced to prescribe rules of conduct that induce a systematic obedience even to wrong choices or bad decisions. Nonetheless, this may lead to compromise with the other partners: each stakeholder looking for their own interest and benefit.

However, loyalty to the *Tutelle*'s action and command is very often belittled to a simple case of administering routine that plagues the entire administrative structure. Universities 'function' with routines that help the leader accomplish the recurrent tasks organizations perform. Managing through routinization is the main criticism voiced by certain stakeholders, because it is opposed to innovation. It is true that university leaders face a dilemma that pushes them to decide upon their own competence or by order to try to introduce innovation, when in fact the whole educational entity is plagued by obsolete and out-of-date relations and processes. Indeed, organizational routine is so strong that it presents an insurmountable practice that paradoxically presents stability in an opaque set. This is why innovative processes to such a state of affairs send the wrong message: uncertainty of what is to be or inadequacy of the proposed change. Routine as understood by those concerned has negative connotations that may mean inertia (Hannan & Freeman, 1983), instability, inflexibility (Gersick & Hackman, 1990), even routine and stagnation. One adds that routines may paradoxically mean good practices and habits. In any case, it is continuity in a negative sense that means in fact going counter change. This is how lay people describe bureaucracy:

an administrative plague inherited from French colonization. In such a case, the leaders are overwhelmed by a system that does not help adaptability to new situations or reactivity to innovative undertakings. One feels that the opposed meaning suggested by a number of researchers (Feldman & Rafaeli, 2002) is unlikely to happen to/in any university that follows orders to build up a workflow that makes all partners feel secure. In this case, is routine not a brake to bringing innovation to a system or an organized set? Does routine provide a stepping board to innovation or reform? Our hypothesis is that routine as practised at university level lacks so much professionalism that it cannot provide the necessary background for a relaxing process of innovation universities are looking for. In fact, the organizational leadership is hostage of routine, felt like stagnation that kills innovation, slows down things and develops by dint of time forces of inertia that will block the planned changes brought to an ailing HE system.

Because the university partners seldom refer to official instructions or code (CUED), they have developed an idea of the missions of the leader dealing principally with the organization of learning. Consequently, the leaders try to create a community of learning in charge of the environmental and organizational factors, at least theoretically. By doing this, they hope to guarantee the flexibility of the training structures by establishing standards and controlling the performance of all stakeholders and thus, providing quality education that is the ultimate aim of the reform. But, there is quite a distance between this idealization of a profession that is attacked from all sides, to the point where a professor labels a large fringe of the university teachers 'false scholars' who are 'in the direction and management functions, who have not allowed the formation of an elite politically distanced and independent from politicized exploitation' (Khaoua, 2019, p. 10). This is why leadership styles are not of a single type. One hypothesis is that leaders adapt themselves to the context they are in by considering all possibilities, the people they are involved with, the goals to attain, the moment and urgency of the decision. Therefore, between loyalty to the institution and mimetic routine, if not apathy, the educational leader is not ready to innovate since his mission is to be pedagogically efficient even if he does not want to change or innovate.

6 The Micropolitical Realities of the Algerian University: Challenges and Perspectives

Known Algerian researchers and university teachers (Chitour, 2000; Kouloughli, 2017; Mebtoul, 2013; Dourari, 2003; Tessa, 2017) have mentioned a sombre perspective for the future of the university due to the politicians' marginalization of the university as a milieu of creation and critical thinking. On the other hand, the aforementioned 'false scholars' are ready:

> [to] invest the partisan political field, while putting forward their quality and their academic ranks, but more, they ignore all ethics when they know the reality of the crisis, the adopted and counterproductive policies participating in its rootedness and its exacerbation without reacting, criticizing publicly, resigning from their political and administrative functions, not to condone. Thus, they confine their knowledge and their mission as intellectuals and academics first and foremost to a politician tool, ignoring any criticism of the 'master.' (Khaoua, March 2019, p. 10)

Reforms, between such hands, are bound to fail. Indeed, officials seem to attract all sorts of criticism from all partners, even their peers because of their total submission to the hierarchy. For this reason, an autonomous group of teachers and researchers recently published an announcement in a newspaper (El Watan, May 6, 2018, p. 2) stating that in HE, "primacy, so often given to administrative logic to the detriment of pedagogy and science, trivialize daily the untimely decisions of bureaucrats who, assured of their impunity, believe they are omnipotent". It is also true that social sciences and humanities are considered the poor relations when opposed to the 'hard sciences' (medicine, physics, maths, etc.) to the point where university rectors are often nominated among teachers with these specialities, establishing in this way a two-tiered university. This feature of the Algerian university is here to stay. Decision-makers have shown and are still showing their bias by dividing the university community into the 'useful' and the 'insignificant'.

If the leadership styles that have been chosen by the respondents to the questionnaire were mostly geared towards a role of a clerk, it is because strict followers are likely not to be bothered by the *Tutelle*. Universities are still waiting for the visionary, the trendsetter. However, one is still wondering if this is not in the realm of the impossible, considering the many exogenous factors that dictate their principles of management (globalization, internationalization of higher education, student/teacher mobility, etc.). If the reform suffered from lack of financial means, ineffective management strategies, and non-discriminatory university access of large student cohorts, genuine leadership is missing most. Less populist and uncompromising figures are not legion. Rectors, deans and department heads are often negotiating their job stability[17] against the ministry's demand for social peace with students. This is why there must be a rethink of the notion of leader-subordinate relationship structure doing away with the century-old authoritarian leadership style, the ongoing idea among university partners of the '*chikh*' (in Arabic the learned, the wise). An idea that is utterly in opposition to the notion of autonomy and an obstacle to responsible leadership and the result is that '… the system has favoured a kind of unhealthy laziness. This comfort of the intellectuals has backfired on them' (Miliani, 1995, p. 27).

Universities need to work towards a non-hierarchical leadership that empowers all stakeholders at a stage or another in order to start conquering their share in the internationalization of HE. Organizational leadership cannot always be in total command to impose its say. Besides, routine as much as innovations must be managed in a way that allows people to become actors of their own fate and not waiting for the other, the leader to fail or show signs of despair when faced with the disorganized settings they have to bring change and order to. This is why: 'to go into an advanced mode of governance requires from the University to undergo its own transformation and be accountable to their constituents by submitting itself at all levels and at any time to the evaluation process' (Zaid, 2018, p. 18). This entrepreneurial approach to governance is not yet a feasible idea in today's Algeria. The massive spread of higher education cannot guarantee quality education nor can it facilitate the work by educational leadership. Leaders are caught between the hammer (the governmental populist policies towards university registration) and the anvil (a plethora of staff and increasing students' cohorts). Nevertheless, '… basically, it is the politician who must free the initiatives within the academic institution before it collects its due of autonomy and its share in the multifaceted development of the country. Otherwise, the University will be in a perpetual humming and/or in the more or less appropriate implementation of imported models not assimilated and ecologically in contradiction with invariants, traits and features of its identity' (Author, 2017, p. 147). Tomorrow's leaders are yet to emerge from an environment in dire need of stability where students will not be decision-takers but partners. Are we not talking of a game of collective make-believe, where teachers are the first victims of unethical behaviors from all sides, and where educational leadership is the outcome of negotiations in the corridors of power?

Notes

1 The LMD reform came first to remould HE in order to guarantee quality formations, while meeting legitimate social demands for access to higher training. It aimed at achieving a true osmosis with the socio-economic environment and at developing the mechanisms of adaptation to the evolutions of jobs, and by consolidating its cultural mission by promoting

2. universal values. The Reform was thus designed for improved student professional insertion, lifelong learning, autonomy of university, and the opening of the university to the world of science and technology.

2. A semi-structured interview was designed and organized with 12 university teachers holding various administrative posts. They had to react freely to nine questions but suggested also other options.

3. I wish to thank Professor Hadj Miliani, University of Mostaganem, for his help with the interviews.

4. The HE system consists of 50 universities; 13 university centers; 20 higher national schools; 10 schools for higher education; 11 teacher training schools, 2 annexes.

5. Nationwide, there are about 11 national student associations.

6. Overall, fourteen specialist domains were targeted: law & political sciences, foreign languages & letters, Arabic language & literature, mathematics & computing, sciences of the matter, sciences & technology, natural and life sciences, sciences of the earth and the universe; economic management and commercial sciences, Islamic sciences; architecture urbanism and the town professions, science and technique of physical and sports activities.

7. Question four asked about their vision of the reform, some said it was a mission (3), other declared it was an obligation (6), and a burden (2). One even added, "Itis a bad answer to a real problem".

8. Here is a sample of several alarmist press titles: 'La réforme LMD et l'université algérienne: les vrai enjeux' (in *Liberté*, 24/04/2004); 'Le LMD, une question de moyens' (in *Horizons*, 7/11/2008); 'Le LMD dans la tourmente' (in *L'Echo d'Oran*, 11/01/2012) ; 'Le LMD, un nid de problèmes' (in *El Watan* (03/12/2014) ; 'LMD, les limites d'un système' (in *Le Quotidien d'Oran*, 13/01/2016) ; 'La descente aux enfers de l'université algérienne' (in *Middle East Eye*, 24/09/2017).

9. Asked whether they considered themselves as leaders, 3 said yes, 8 no. One went on to say that, he was only responsible for its implementation.

10. As defined by OECD: "the possibility to define independently its own standards and values for teaching, research and management of the institutions" (Ghouati, 2012).

11. One can venture to suggest that in the early days of independence until the 1980/1990, the university officials did not have high degrees. Besides, the one-party system was always making sure that its members got the highest posts in HE while higher degrees-holders were kept aside busy teaching and doing research.

12. "Power in the sphere of education is understood as the capacities and/or strategies generated by individuals or groups of persons, to achieve or influence the accomplishment of tasks or actions for or by education" (Author, 2003, p. 62).

13. "National student associations play an important role by helping organize students' responses to change and by exercising an efficacious power of lobbying in the name of students at a national and international levels" (Benstaali, 2013, p. 2)

14. To Question 3, the respondents admitted they were authoritarian (8), others were not (3). One even reacted differently by saying that he was responsible but exercising authority.

15. Conférence Nationale des Universités ; conférences régionales des universités (East, West, Center).

16. Question seven revealed differences of opinion between those who believed that in order to succeed, they had to rely on their competence (7), their leadership (3), and their courage (0). Two were only too happy to follow their superiors' orders.

17. Several researchers have, playing on words, talked about *"la lutte des places"* (struggle for position instead of *'la lutte des classes'*: class struggle) to describe the 'scramble' between teachers for administrative and political positions in the system.

References

Benghabrit-Remaoun, N., & Rabahi-Senouci, Z. (2009). Le système LMD (Licence-Master-Doctorat) en Algérie: de l'illusion de la nécessité du choix de l'opportunité. *JHEA/RESA, 7*(2).

Benstaali, B. (2013). Evaluation de Modes de Gouvernance Universitaire; Etude comparative des universités Européennes et Algériennes, La Gouvernance Universitaire, Analyses comparées des Universités Maghrébines. *Oran: Ed. Dar El Gharb, 2013*, 213–228.

Bessadi, N. (2017, September 24). La descente aux enfers de l'université algérienne. *Middle East Eye*.

Blase, J., & Anderson, G. (1995). *The micropolitics of educational leadership: From control to empowerment*. Cassell.

Bourdieu, P., & Passeron, J. C. (1970). *La Reproduction – éléments pour une théorie du système d'enseignement*. les éditions de Minuit.

Charte d'éthique et de déontologie universitaire. (2010). MESRS.

Chitour, C. E. (2000). *Le système éducatif algérien: à l'heure de l'internet et de la mondialisation*. Marinoor.

Dourari, A. (2003). *Les malaises de la société algérienne, crise de langue et crise d'identité*. Casbah.

Duclos, A. M. (2015). La résistance au changement: un concept désuet et inapproprié en éducation. *Psychologie et éducation, 34*, 2015-1.

Feldman, M. S., & Rafaeli, A. (2002, December). Organizational routines as a source of connections and understandings. *Journal of Management Studies*.

Gersick, C. J. G., & Hackman, J. R. (1990). Habitual routines in task-performing teams. *Organizational Behavior and Human Decision Processes, 47*, 65–97.

Ghouati, N. (2012, Juin). La dépossession. Réformes, enseignement supérieur et pouvoirs au Maghreb. *Revue des Mondes musulmans et de la Méditerranée, 131*.

Hannan, M. T., & Freeman, J. (1984). Structural inertia and organizational change. *American Sociology Review, 49*, 149–64.

Hirschman, A. O. (1970). *Exit, voice and loyalty: Responses to decline in firms, organizations and states*. Harvard University Press.

Hoyle, E. (1982). Micropolitics of educational organisations. *Educational Management and Administration, 10*, 87–98.

Khaoua, N. (2019, March 16). Crise systémique, conscience populaire et trahison des clercs en Algérie. *Le Quotidien d'Oran*.

Kouloughli, L. (2017). *Une université algérienne au prisme d'un de ses départements*. El Othmania.

Mebtoul, M. (2013). *La citoyenneté en question*. Dar El Adib.

Miliani, H. (1995, Mars). La culture face à la terreur. *Télérama: Algérie*, 26–29.

Miliani, M. (2003, April). Arabisation of higher education in Algeria: linguistic centralism vs. democratisation. *International Journal of Contemporary Sociology, 40*(1), 55–74.

Miliani, M. (2016). L'enseignement de l'éthique à l'université: approche globale. *Les Dossiers du Gree. Série 3. Éthique en éducation et en formation. Questions d'éthique et de formation en éducation et en santé.* www.gree.uqam.ca

Miliani, M. (2017). La réforme LMD: un problème d'implémentation. *Insaniyat, 75–76*, 129–148.

Miliani, M. (2019, July 9–10). *La résistance des enseignants universitaires à la réforme LMD: Une démarche éthique et responsable?* Paper presented at the Symposium REF 2019, Éthiques et résistances dans les mondes de l'éducation, de la formation et de la santé.

Schön, D. A. (1983). *The reflective practitioner: How professionals think in action.* Temple Smith.

Tessa, A. (2017). *L'impossible éradication: l'enseignement du français en Algérie.* L'Harmattan.

Zaid, I. A. (2018, January 6–7). Le système de l'enseignement supérieur algérien: réformer l'esprit plutôt que les formes? *El Watan.*

CHAPTER 7

Digitally Equipped: Reshaping Educational Leadership and Management in Italy

Paolo Landri and Danilo Taglietti

Abstract

In this chapter, we will focus on the digital turn in educational leadership in Italy. After a long-lasting period when educational reforms were oriented to introduce methodologies, tools and practices from the New Public Management (Grimaldi, Landri, & Serpieri, 2016), there has been recently a decisive turn towards the introduction of 'The Digital' as the new molar agency (Deleuze, 1988) around which educational practices are organized. Educational leadership does not get out of this tendency and has again become a privileged object of government reforms. By drawing on ANT and Foucauldian perspectives, our work envisages tracing how the New Public Management and the digital turn are reshaping practices of educational leadership and management. The chapter is based on an extensive set of empirical researches on education reform (Grimaldi & Barzanò, 2014; Grimaldi, Landri, & Serpieri, 2016; Grimaldi & Serpieri, 2013; Serpieri, 2013) and recent investigations on the introduction and the impact of the digital governance of education in Italy.

Keywords

Actor-Network Theory (ANT) – Foucault – attachment – assemblages – school leadership – school leader presences – digital turn – digital governance of education – New Public Management (NPM) – Italy – school leader subjectivations

1 Introduction

In this chapter, we will focus on the digital turn in educational leadership in Italy. After a long-lasting period when educational reforms were oriented to introduce methodologies, tools and practices from the New Public Management (Grimaldi, Landri, & Serpieri, 2016), there has recently been a decisive turn towards the introduction of 'The Digital' as the new molar agency

(Deleuze, 1988) around which educational practices are organized. Educational leadership does not get out of this tendency and has again become a privileged object of government reforms.

By drawing on ANT and Foucauldian perspectives, our work envisages tracing how the New Public Management and the digital turn are reshaping practices of educational leadership and management. The chapter is based on an extensive set of empirical research on education reform (Grimaldi & Barzanò, 2014; Grimaldi, Landri, & Serpieri, 2016; Grimaldi & Serpieri, 2013; Serpieri, 2013) and recent investigations on the introduction and the impact of the digital governance of education in Italy. We will highlight how the practice of educational leadership is changing and is becoming an emergent human-paper-digital assemblage. We will see how the work of school leaders in Italy is immersed in a network of attachment where digital platforms, software, and applications are playing an increasing role. At the same time, we will also illustrate how school leaders are not 'passive recipients' or 'cultural dopes' of the digital governance of education: they reply, surprisingly and in a creative way, to the digitalization and datafication of education paving the way in practice to the development of autonomous subjectivities.

The chapter includes a theoretical and an empirical section. Theoretically, we will draw on a vocabulary trying to combine ANT and After (Law & Hassard, 1999) and Foucault: (a) to disentangle the concrete assemblages of humans and nonhumans in the contemporary educational leadership; (b) to underline the relevance of the processes of subjectivation to illustrate educational leadership as emerging from a network of attachment. Empirically, we will offer an empirical description of the general changing conditions of the work of school leaders. We will pay attention to the concatenation of paper, humans and digital that is reshaping educational leadership and management and on the emergent processes of subjectivation, through several on-going ethnographies in some schools in South Italy. We will finally summarize our chapter by illustrating how the current trends are producing novel actor-networks and the emergence of new subjectivities.

2   Where Foucalt Meets ANT, or ANT Rediscovering the Foucauldian Heritage

Drawing on Actor-Network Theory to analyze educational leadership and management could appear to some extent, a paradox. By definition, the vocabulary of ANT invites to the decentring from humans and considering the materialities of practice, to shift attention to how objects, technologies and things make the social. ANT undermines the role generally attributed to the humans in the classic and the contemporary literature on leadership, both in management and education studies. Is it possible to use ANT as a companion to study educational leadership and management dynamics? In this chapter, we will make a trial in this direction, by proposing to move to 'ANT and After' framework and, partly, recovering the Foucauldian heritage (Law & Hassard, 1999). Also, Foucault has often been considered to hold an anti-humanist position, since when he argued for the death of the man (Foucault, 2005) and also for dismissing the author function (Foucault, 1981). Despite this official reception of his thought, Deleuze (2006) underlines that Foucault was interested not in subjects as reified entities; but in those processes that shape subjectivities' form: the processes of subjectivation.

In making this transgressive assemblage, we think we are in line with the open-ended characteristic of ANT, which characterizes itself, since the beginning, as a collective endeavour that hybridizes many collateral lines of reflection and investigation (feminism, post-structuralism, post-humanism, etc.). We also reprise a crucial shift in its historical trajectory, when the perspective opened in fields of research other than the social study of science and technology, and the internal debate led to rethinking the work that has been since realized then (Latour, 1999b; Law, 1998).

However, it should be misleading to convey the idea that classic ANT was not interested in analysing the subject, while in ANT and After there would be more space for this area of research. Suffice to remind the classic investigation of the Pasteurization of France by Bruno Latour (Latour, 1984), and Law's ethnography on dynamic of a scientific laboratory (Law, 1994), where they offered an interesting sociological reading of the dynamics of organizational leadership, paving the way to the spread of ANT in organization studies. In his analysis, Latour described the Pasteur-network, that is the network of items Pasteur was able to associate with, giving him the chance to become an obligatory point of passage – to use an essential concept of ANT-vocabulary – of a process of knowledge accumulation. On the contrary, Law illustrates the multiple reality of the scientific laboratory characterized by the loose association and performance of concurrent modes of ordering, leading to the various modes of enactment of organizational leadership. On his own, also, Foucault had always been interested in the production of subjects, enhancing a perspective focused on power dynamics. In fact, the docilization of the body in Discipline and Punish (Foucault, 1995) could be considered as a historically rooted analysis of the social production of the 'disciplined form' taken by subjects in the Fordist society.

So, both in Foucault and in ANT, the decentering of the subject was not conducive to a rude materialistic or technological determinism, leading to a radical anti-humanism. It suggests to pay attention: (1) to the human not as an essence, but as a contingent and situated form, and (2) to the entanglement of humans and nonhumans as a critical unit of analysis.

The hyphen in the notion of actor-network, in this sense, is what makes this theoretical sensibility peculiar. 'Humans' and 'nonhumans' are treated as actor-networks (actor *and* network at the same time): in other words as *assemblages*, heterogeneous entities with a syntax. ANT is interested in bringing to the forefront, to understand the logic of association and the processes of making it durable. In the same vein, Foucault is also interested in this syntax, but relying on the ontological principle that it is enmeshed in power dynamics and rules (Peters & Taglietti, 2019), highlighting the strategies of domination through which each subjective-form is affected. In this framework, educational leadership and management are understood not as a personal trait or a model, but as a situated, historical and contingent assemblage of humans and nonhumans aimed at hierarchizing, giving directions, coordinating and controlling schools as organizations. School leadership could be seen as a never complete *action-net*: a collective, powerful, and sometimes contested, composition in practice of human and nonhuman entities.

In the classic ANT, the syntax of this composition is 'network'; the stability of the association assumes the network-form, and the story of the consolidation is told by the network-builder, albeit decentered. There is an insistence on uniformity and convergence as if the shape and the materialization of the social were fixed in a unique configuration. The description of the dynamics of leadership indulges too much on Machiavellian strategy, and the consolidation of patterned relations, with the insistence of production of 'sameness' in regimes of translation. It also resonates with the typical Foucauldian reading of school leadership (Gillies, 2013) as related only to control, surveillance and discipline in the constraints of a power 'dispositif'. No space is left for the emergence and the generation of new competencies, alternative views and the invention and experimentation of new "modes of existence" (Foucault, 2010, p. 3). In practice, the use of the classic ANT and Foucauldian approaches provide a useful description of school leadership as a power assemblage, and how this assemblage is changing over time; it remains silent, however, as to the generative side of the process.

In fact, as Revel (2016) puts it, the process of production of subjects, that Foucault calls subjectivation, is

> a paradoxical process of objectivation that, in turn, entails a series of operation: nomination, identification, circumscription, determination, qualification, hierarchisation, etc. [but also] the way in which a human being is transformed into subject [...] the possibility to unbalance the

chiasm. [That means:] to put to work again what Foucault describes as a 'reciprocal incitation', or as an 'agonism' between power and freedom, or between objectification and autonomous subjectivation. (pp. 166–167)

To grasp this double-sided or chiasmatic aspect of the subjectivation process, we propose to move to ANT and After: in a post-classic ANT scenario, there is a shift to *performativity*. While the vocabulary of ANT focuses on disentangling the assemblage of humans and nonhumans; in ANT and After, the social can inhabit multiple realities, and topologies, and the theory of action is even more problematized. An effect of ANT is that the action is distributed so that it can be drawn attention to materialities, objects and technologies that, in our case, are contributing to the making of school leadership. However, it is still a theory of action that keeps on asking 'who is acting?', by displacing the cognitive capacities of humans to nonhumans.

A useful enlargement, here, is given by the notion of *attachment*, which shifts the attention to the analysis of the configurations of 'what occurs' (Gomart & Hennion, 1999). The notion of *attachment* is a challenge to the relevance of the 'action' in ANT, as it invites to look instead at the 'events'. It draws attention to what makes us act, without assuming a causal determination, or absolute freedom. Instead, *attachment* collapses objects and subjects by directing towards 'bonds to our nearest and dearest, to places, to memberships, to origins – however in 'attachment', the '-ment' says that it has to be made, even if it makes us in return' (Hennion, 2007, 2017). The passage from the notion of 'network' to the concept of 'attachment' (Latour, 1999a) helps to consider in a more sophisticated way the issue of the social emancipation that has been quickly sorted as freedom from all constraints. Also, it has helped ANT to have a vocabulary to analyze new territories of research, like taste, music, and drug addiction where descriptions of subject-networks are required and attention of 'what happens' is essential to underline the emergence of dynamics of subjectivation.

Here, we argue for an analytical split in the concept of attachment that could make it useful for detecting both the power dynamics and the traces of the new emergences that are implied in the shaping of subjectivities: on the one side, 'objectifying attachments' talk about operations of objectivation; on the other side, 'autonomizing attachments' bring to the fore those acts of subjectivation that are partially autonomous from the logics of objectivation. A mix of activity and passivity is visible: subjectivities are made by policy assemblage and, at the same time, by embodying it, they can fold it and could be capable of independent determinations. By looking closely at the network of attachments, it is then possible to describe the enactment of the policy assemblage, that is its constraining and generative instantiations. It is possible to see when it produces expected and routinized functionings through 'objectifying attachments' and when unexpected and unforeseen functionings by envisaging 'autonomizing attachments'.

In the following section, we will put to test our framework by analyzing the new school leadership in Italy. After a general and brief introduction to the policy-making of new school leadership in Italy, we will offer some analysis of how Italian educational leadership and management is becoming a *paper-digital-human assemblage*. Then, we will draw more close attention to the *multiplication of presences of school leaders*, one among the most exciting and emergent processes of subjectivation.

3   New School Leadership in Italy

In the last two decades, the Italian education system has been interested in the process of reculturing intended to implement the logic, the discourses and the practices of the New Public Management (Gunther, Grimaldi, Hall, & Serpieri, 2016). The reform of the school autonomy, the decentralization of the system, the shift in the financial management towards limited forms of responsibility for results, the introduction of audit and performance management technologies and, the changing direction in the personnel management, more and more linked to performance and incentive schemes, have been aimed at the reorientation of institutional configuration of an education governance historically characterized by bureaucratic and welfarist regimes.

The transformations have interested the discourses, the technologies of governance and the subjects of the system, which have been redirected and reoriented towards the consolidation of a regime of governance by standards, where performance standards (here operationalized in terms of learning outcomes) are meant to increase the efficacy and the efficiency of the education system.

Of particular interest, here, are the policies having as a target the headteacher. Since the reform of school autonomy in 1997, headteachers changed its role. In the new landscape, they were given a new identity and title. Formerly 'headteachers', they were named 'managers'. Accordingly, they were interested in a new training course, inspired by managerialism and leadership. They were asked to assume a leading role in the organization of the school, by expanding their activities in managerial and educational managing areas. School Managers are expected to use tools like planning, target setting and data collection, in an institutional framework that was paradoxically crossed by trends towards decentralization and, at the same time, renewed attempts to reinforce the centralism of the Ministry. Schools and headteachers are required to act in a quasi-market mode, while still enclosed in a classic bureaucratic chain of command.

A 'war of discourses' between bureaucracy, managerial, professional and democratic principles feeds unsolved contradictions and dilemmas in everyday life of headteachers: still involved in the legacy of the past configurations of the educational governance, they are not entirely aligned, regardless the rhetorics, to a managerial practice business-like oriented (Serpieri, 2009). Thus, the essential feature of the school leader is the 'hybrid headteacher' form, where competing institutional logics are at stake and are required to be combined and recomposed in practice (Gunther et al., 2016).

The unresolved production of the new identity, in turn, mirrors a complex reshaping of the materiality of the headteacher, which is troubled by the introduction of new objects, like education plans, public service charts, self-evaluation reports, performance standards, educational systems, websites. They are ontologically incomplete objects, as they expect to be fixed and defined by deliberations taken at the level of schools (Landri, 2009). A complicated and unfinished re-assemblage of humans and nonhumans occurs without leading to a stable configuration, as it is evident in the long-lasting attempts to re-introduce forms of evaluation for headteachers, and in the several policies aimed at reinforcing the school managerial role through the expansion of middle management (Grimaldi & Barzanò, 2014; Serpieri, 2009).

The new reforms are accompanied by parallel and to some extent, epochal changes in the technologies of governance. School autonomy has implied a restructuring of the organizational field and, in particular, of the informative system (Landri & Serpieri, 2004). The new development of digital technologies is paving the way for the progressive decline of analogue technologies (Souto-Otero & Beneito-Montagut, 2016). Paper that was important in the bureaucratic setting is made less important, and there is a shift (not completely fulfilled) towards the 'digital'. We are witnessing the emergence of a new regime of visibility of education practice: the governance of education becomes increasingly digital as platforms, applications, software, data are seen and implemented as the 'necessary' companions (the smart 'partners') of education policy and practice. There is no policy without a platform, or software, that gives due support and directs the implementation stage. At the same time, there is the requirement for education practice to be more and more imbricated in digital media. We have accordingly an acceleration of datafication of education, that already started well before, with a clear orientation towards standard-based reform, as an effect of the traceability made possible by digital technologies. Educational professions become more digital and so educational leadership and management; notably, the digitalization is meant as inevitable and is rarely problematized. A rhetoric of necessity and an enlightening perspective on new technologies are dominant as if they were neutral and technical fixes of modern education.

To problematize this optimistic scenario, and also to understand how it merges with the war of discourses that have characterized the changing governance of education in Italy, we are realizing some *multi-sited ethnographies* (Landri, 2019; Taglietti, 2019) with the aim of understanding what is happening to the work of school leaders in a landscape characterized by datafication and digitalization, and how new human-digital attachments are developing in practice. In our case, the methodology consisted basically of following the actors and in the ethnographical principle of making the familiar strange. We realized interviews (to headteachers and teachers with a role in managerial tasks) and in-site observations of educational leadership and management practices. We were able to describe educational leadership and management in four schools for one scholastic year. We could then zoom out and zoom in of practice in the stage of analysis (Nicolini, 2010). In what follows, by zooming-out, we will give an illustration of how the digital is changing the work of school leaders. Then, by zooming in on a concrete concatenation of educational management, we will present how the fabrication of new school leadership can lead, in practice, to the multiplication of the presences of the school leader.

4 School Leadership as a Paper-Human-Digital Assemblage

In zooming out of the practice, our ethnographies describe how Italian school leaders are invited to become *paper-human-digital assemblages*. To some extent, and partly reflecting the specific regulation of the educational management in this country, they are asked to be a *collective accomplishment*. The materiality of the paper and the technology of writing associated with the paper do not disappear from the scene of the everyday work of the school leader; however, it is not important as it was underlined in the bureaucratic discourse. The policy of de-materialization, a word used to mean the reduction of paper and at the same time, the need for an increasing digitalization of documents, acts of direction, circulars, decisions. There is rather a shifting out from the paper to their digital version that can be more easily transferred, stored, and shared. Even the signature of the school leader is now translated in a digital protocol as it is in the electronic signature: this requires new infrastructures and protocols, with the collaboration of private companies, and new objects, like one-time password, software and other security applications. Huge investments in the digitalization have transformed the act of signature that is a key aspect of the managerial work, as it authorizes, validates and makes effective a decision. Instruments like smartphones and computers are now at the core of the school leaders' tasks and, more in general, of the educational professionals. They are ubiquitous as they are the vehicles of new attachments: both are relevant actors, as they help a school leader in getting the work done, since they are useful to giving directions, realizing coordination, trailing the connection, having data and information at a distance, that is to build up a presence in the bodily absence. By smartphones, and notably with the creation of a WhatsApp group, school leaders can be in touch with everybody. Moreover, school leaders have to deal with a plethora of platforms, software and digital formations they can have access via computers or smartphones. These are the materialization of the attachments with the Ministry of Education, with its central and peripheral offices, with public agencies (like INVALSI, the National Agency of Evaluation) and other national and regional authorities, with the teachers of their schools, with the parents, and with the overall public audience, as in the case of school websites, and pages on the social media, like Facebook and Twitter. Each platform requires a profile: therefore, school leaders have a multiplicity of digital avatars. As the reform of the school autonomy meant mostly a de-concentration, more than an effective decentralization of power and competencies from the Ministry of Education, school leaders were attributed additional managerial tasks in public procurement, in the management of the personnel, in financial accounting, and in workplace safety. Most of these tasks entail access to platforms and digital formations resulting in a multiplication of the digital presence of the same school leader (for example ARAN, ENTRATEL, PERLAPA, Passweb INPS, Acquisti in Rete PA), and in an imbalance of the management tasks in comparison with the educational side of the role. Even in that case, however, education policies materialize in the forms of platforms and software. Self-evaluation reports, plans for the educational offer, plans for improvement, portfolios for the assessment of the school leaders and electronic registers are digitalized. Digitalization, in that respect, offers assistance and helps in getting the work done. At the same time, they are not neutral as they have politics. In the case of the self-evaluation report, for example, some specific aspects of the curriculum are privileged, forcing schools to comply with national standards. In so doing, furthermore, they direct attention on the most visible and measurable items of educational practice, leaving in the background some qualitative, and therefore elusive and non-measurable, parts. They embody therefore an 'epistemology of seeing' that translates the complexity of education in a narrow framework, putting an overemphasis on competencies like literacy and numeracy, or performance standards as lists of indicators and benchmarks define them. They also enact a space of commensurability among schools, feeding a logic of competitiveness and quasi-market, as in some digital platforms, like 'Eduscopio' that are explicitly oriented to school choice at the upper secondary school by ranking school performance. The electronic register provides important software for school management. This latter substituted the paper printed registers where teachers took note of the attendance, kept summaries on the lectures, added the marks for the school assessment, and inserted all the relevant information about the everyday life of a classroom (including penalties for the student in case of misbehavior). In practice, the electronic register expands the role of the paper register and archives additional information, permitting at the same time, with several requirements, to give updated information about the classroom activities and furnish 'real-time' information to parents and students (For example, it provides information on the presence of students in the classroom, and results of the assessment). The register allows as well to prepare the collective decision on the mid-term and the final time of the school year. There is no a unique software that can perform these tasks: private companies have developed several applications, and each school leader, together with the teaching staff opts for the most convenient solution. The market, in that respect, is not completely open, as there are a limited number of companies and accordingly, of available technical solutions. Of course, school leader assemblages are made not only by paper and digital matter; it is a human-nonhuman concatenation, where the attachment with bodies is very relevant. This leads to consider, on the one hand, the bodily presence of the school leader and, on the other hand, the bodies of the school teachers that are delegated educational leadership and management tasks. The reform of school autonomy led to the expansion of middle management. More and more school teachers are chosen as direct delegates by the school leader and elected by the Council of each school to help in school management and to contribute to the school organizational ordering. This proliferation is telling and has been triggered by the need to contextualize educational policies, like the prevention of early school, leaving, the integration of students with a migrant background, the special education for disabled, etc This expansion means a flattening of the school hierarchy, and an increasing need of coordination and communication that feeds a demand of digital solutions (use social network like WhatsApp; cloud computing, like Dropbox; video conferencing, using Skype for example).

5 The Multiplication of School Leader Presences

By zooming in on concrete assemblages, our ethnographies illustrate that the imbrication in the digital is so significant that the proliferation of digital profiles of school leaders can permit the multiplication of his/her presences. He/she can be 'there' with his/her digital avatars while not being bodily co-present. School leadership, in another way, can emerge in 'hybrid production of presence(s)' (Fairhurst & Cooren, 2009).

The multiplication of presences consists of a series of attachments which does not suppress nor automatize school leadership. Instead, it presents the leader's subjectivity as a new configuration constituted in practice through a net of attachments among many human and non-human, both analogical and digital elements. The situatedness and contingency of this series of attachments not only helps non-human elements in producing humans but also opens up the opportunity for humans for making themselves differently. Following the transgressive assemblage between ANT and Foucault proposed in the theoretical section, we will highlight this chiasmatic process through the concept of attachment and its analytical split between the objectifying attachment and the autonomizing attachment.

The multiplication of presences happens, in particular, in the main areas invested by the proliferation of digital platforms aimed at presenting projects, but also at collecting data, information, and documentation on the selected financed school activities.

In Italy, since the 1990s, the constant and progressive reduction of the funding granted by the government to the public educational system has been accompanied by a proliferation of opportunities to access extraordinary funding. The mechanism designed to obtain money from these channels, over time, has reinforced a now permanent link between the design of educational projects and the possibility to concur in receiving European Structural Funds (PON) or regional funds of the National Operative Program (POR). This mechanism plans: a call for projects on specific issues by national or regional government; the drawing up of a thematic educational project by the school; the wait for the list of the winner projects; and the implementation of the project, to be done in parallel with some intermediate and final accounting activities regarding the attending pupils, the experts involved, the costs sustained, the timing, and so on.

To illustrate how the multiplication of presence may occur, we will describe in detail an episode taken from one of our ethnographies. In particular, we followed the reporting and accounting activities that a school leader is requested to accomplish nowadays. The school educational staff, in the previous months, designed many projects in order to answer a call for projects by the regional government for the assignment of POR fundings through the policy "Living-School", an annual program which finances initiatives aimed at the quality improvement of the regional school system. After securing the fundings, they engaged in the implementation of the designed educational activities. Then, the headteacher received a friendly reminder by the competent regional office in order to complete the reporting and accounting activities on the digital platform named "SURF", within 30 days from the end of the project. This reminder started the attachment of human and non-human elements that we are now going to present.

In the administrative offices of the school, one of the administrative clerks is sitting at her desk, furnished with a desktop personal computer, and surfs the web. She digits on the keyboard "www.google.it" in the address bar of the web browser. Once on the google website, she digits "surf regione Campania" in the research bar. Then, the list of search results appears. The first result is the SURF website, while the second one is a pdf document named "SURF's user manual". She tries to access the SURF website. The browser's address bar moves to the new address: "https://surf.regione.campania.it/surf". "How could I remember such a difficult internet address? There are many non-sense letters, points, columns, signs of every kind. Fortunately, I can go to google and write there everything I need for going to the website" (Clerk1). Shifting away from the difficult technicalities of an attachment with the specific internet address, the clerk engages with the user-friendly semantics of google, which gives the clerk access to the regional platform. This objectifying attachment with Google makes SURF reachable by the clerk.

Anyway, this is not enough. The browser's address bar moves to the new address, but no webpage is loaded. After some minutes, the clerk reloads the page. The SURF webpage does not load again. She tries once more. Same result: no page loaded. "It may be the internet connection ... or the platform, who can know it? It does not work. Well, we will try again tomorrow" (Clerk1). The autonomizing attachment between the internet connection and the website makes the clerk suddenly desist from her work.

The next day, everything is working well. When Google shows the list, the clerk looks at the second result, the user manual of the SURF platform: "And then ... they also made a user guide, you know. Moreover, there they show all that you can do with the platform ... Well, I think so. Nevertheless, no one of us was able to read it: it is unintelligible. We have to do everything by ourselves" (Clerk1). It's enough to read some lines from the 182 pages of the document in order to agree that the autonomizing attachment between the SURF manual and the users makes them unexpectedly self-taught users: "The navigational logic behind the S.U.R.F. responds to the principles of usability and of ergonomics, in response to the multiple needs of users" (SURF Manual, p. 6).

When the SURF home page is loaded, the clerk proceeds with the login. She digits the institutional e-mail of the school and a password. Once logged-in, the operator is recognized as the headteacher of the school: "Yes, we all use the headteacher account. Indeed, we tried to set different accounts for each one of us, but sometimes they work, some other times they do not work ... So we prefer to use the only one account that permits us to do everything" (Clerk1). The objectifying attachment between the log-in and the account settings makes the headteacher present and performing digital reporting and accounting activities even when she is not in front of the screen.

At this point, the clerk stops her work at the pc: the connection works, the platform works, "Well, now we have to prepare the documents" (Clerk1). After about 20 minutes, the office is full of people: the vice-headteacher, the Director of General and Administrative Services (DSGA), two other administrative clerks. While the desks in the office are full of paper: binders of documents, white sheets, pencils, printed papers.

The first accounting issue faced pertains to the payments to the experts. Each expert involved in the educational projects was paid through a bank wire transfer. The platform requires, for each project, to upload the transfer order for each expert. While one clerk is sitting in front of the screen and engages with the platform which makes her select one of the projects from which to start; the DSGA takes in hand the list of the experts involved in that project, which is to say, mobilizing the concept of attachment previously illustrated: the DSGA attaches through her hands with a printed paper with the list of the experts. This list allows her reading the name of the expert, the amount of the transfer and the date. Another clerk attaches with the project binder, which makes him look for the printed order of payment. If he finds it, the clerk at the pc attaches with a folder on the pc that makes her upload the pdf file named with the expert name and the date of the wire transfer.

On the contrary, if he does not find the printed order of payment in the binder, then the pc makes the clerk in front of it executing the following operations: going to the bank website, recalling from the database the missing order of payment, making a screenshot of the order of payment, pasting it on a blank word page, printing the word page on a pdf file and saving it in the specific folder, uploading the pdf on the platform and then printing the pdf on the printer, so that the other clerk can file it in the project binder. In the meantime, the last clerk uses a pencil and a paper that help him taking note of the total amount of each transfer. At the end of this complicated procedure, a calculator helps him calculating the total amount of the transfers for the experts involved in the project. The pencil allows him to write this final amount on the paper, and the platform aids the other clerk to insert the numbers composing this final amount in the specific required field. All of these can be considered as objectifying attachments: despite the digital or analogic "nature" of the non-human elements involved, we can underline that they produce the ordinary accomplishment of the tasks expected by the accounting practice. The analogic listing of the experts and the paper-and-pencil calculation of the expenses, attached with the digital production and uploading of the documents, make the SURF platform functioning as a reporting device and make the school an accounted organization.

When the reporting of the payments ends, many people leave the office, and only the vice-headteacher and one administrative clerk remain in front of the screen. The clerk moves to the second accounting issue: information about the pupils attending each project. She browses the platform and goes to the "manage recipients" section. Here the platform makes them visualize a list of 10 pupils per page, categorized for fiscal code, citizenship and participating status ("active/inactive"). By clicking on each name, the platform performs the visualizing and managing of the registry with the social and educational information of the pupils. Here, many fields for each pupil have to be filled in. Some of them are undisputable: e-mail, fiscal code, participating status, last degree, research-project title, and so on. While some other labels are somewhat misleading and, in the attachment with the clerk, make her being confused: working status, role, vulnerability group, research-project discipline. She asks the vice-headteacher what she should choose among the limited alternatives of the drop-down menu:

> look at this list: 'political science, humanities, medical sciences, literacy, earth sciences, chemistry, biomedical sciences, public health sciences, Economics and Statistics Department, not applicable ...'. Which could be the discipline of this project, named 'freely in the natural environment – hippotherapy / the limelight 1 / song of the sirens 2 / three colors for two flags / English 1'? (Clerk1)

The autonomizing attachment between the vice-headteacher and the unintelligible user's manual we saw above makes him answer in a self-taught way:

> maybe these disciplines concern the projects made by universities: 'LivingSchool' is a comprehensive policy, handed to many public and private entities. We are only a comprehensive school: I think you have to select 'not applicable'. (Vice-headteacher)

We can see here how the platform was designed to make each school collect as much data as possible about the attendants, in order to profile them precisely, and how, at the same time, there was a completely unexpected interruption of this function through the unforeseen folding of the vice-headteacher. He was neither an opponent nor critic of the platform design, but nevertheless, the attachment in which he is produced makes him interrupt the flow of profiling, opting out towards a different and hastier understanding of the aims of this section of the platform.

6   Conclusions

Educational leadership is considered as a key variable for the intervention and modification of whole educational systems. In Italy, this approach materialized in several policies that, since the end of the past century, have tried to improve schools' added value and pupils' outcomes by targeting school leaders, making them autonomous, responsible, managerially oriented and, at last, digitally equipped. In this chapter, we tried to study this long-lasting policy mixing 'ANT and After' and Foucault. Studying leadership from a perspective that de-centers the subject, dismissing it from the throne of the Prometric owner of the action, is the chance to *re-find* it at the end of a process of production: the effect of a process of subjectivation. Subjectivation emerges in a network of attachment of bits and pieces, human and non-human, analogic and digital, which in turn objectifies or autonomizes the subject.

Our empirical analysis underlines at least three aspects on the interplay between leadership, digitalization and dynamics of power.

First of all, leadership is not a personal trait of a human individual, but a subjective configuration that emerges via a network of attachments. By focusing on events, such as accounting and reporting, we were quite surprised to discover that the platform presupposes a leader and seems to be enacted by a specific individual (the headteacher, whose account is in use). In practice, it was made operative by multiple attachments of different humans (many: not the headteacher!) and non-humans, both analogic and digital. There is a need, therefore, to complexify the standard approach and look for leadership not in a single human, but in the situated set of relations that are contingently put in practice in the making of daily organizational events.

Secondly, while digitalization is often presented as a pervasive system for surveillance and control (Zuboff, 2019), our research shows that this control is an effect which emerges from situated and contingent practices. Moreover, the concepts of 'objectifying attachment' and 'autonomizing attachment' may help to underline the entanglement of practices. There is a strong effect of surveillance which emerges from objectifying attachments. The identification of the headteacher as the operator who makes the accounting, although he was not bodily there, is a case of surveillance and control: the attachment between the log-in procedure and the account settings situates him as the only one responsible for the entire event. However, there are also other effects. Firstly, there is the attachment between the 'non-working' connection and the not-reachable website, which makes accounting a practice dilated over time, postponed and broken. It concurs to make this practice a mere bureaucratic task, although nothing works. Further, there is the attachment between the too many technical platform guide-lines and the users, which become "self-taught users". Here, the difference between the regular functioning of the process and the practices adopted becomes huge, sharply reducing the surveillance that these platforms can push. It also opens up spaces for resistance and dissidence. It is not necessarily a political resistance, but it is an act which makes a difference a practiced possibility (Foucault, 2011).

Finally, according to our analysis, digitalization is a process that concerns the modification of practices. School 'leaders' face a great number of platforms every day: we can say that they could be considered digitalized. However, these platforms are imbricated in a continuous series of shifting and trespassing between the analogic and the digital. The concept of attachment reveals to be useful here as it permits to go beyond the usual argument about the inability of bureaucratic organizations to use the new technologies. It moves the focus from the 'nature' of the elements in play towards the kind of operations that are enabled. The analytical split between objectifying and autonomizing attachment allows to shift further the attention on the linkages between these operations and power dynamics. Where usual functionings forecasted by objectifying attachments succeed to flow undaunted, as much as where deviations by autonomizing attachments suddenly arise, we can find both digital and analogic elements. This permits on the one hand to reconsider the enlightening gaze through which we look at digital innovation as a 'divine gift' (Bourdieu, 1990); while, on the other hand, to take distance from the pessimistic perspective which looks at the digital as a 'new nazism' (Berardi, 2019).

References

Berardi, F. B. (2019). Caos, automa e transumano | Not. *Nero Magazine*.
    https://not.neroeditions.com/nazismo-transumano/
Bourdieu, P. (1990). *Sullo Stato. Corso al Collège de France: 1989–1990* (Vol. 1). Feltrinelli.
Cetina, K. K., & Bruegger, U. (2002). Traders' engagement with markets: A postsocial relationship. *Theory, Culture & Society, 19*(5–6), 161–185. https://doi.org/10.1177/ 026327602761899200

Cova, B., & Cova, V. (2002). Tribal marketing: The tribalisation of society and its impact on the conduct of marketing. *European Journal of Marketing, 36*(5–6), 595–620.
Deleuze, G. (1988) *Foucault*. University of Minnesota Press.
Deleuze, G. (2006). *Foucault* (S. Hand, Ed.). University of Minnesota Press.
Foucault, M. (1981). The order of discourse. In R. Young (Ed.), *Untying the text: A post-structuralist reader* (pp. 48–78). Routledge & Kegan Paul.
Foucault, M. (1995). *Discipline and punish. The birth of the prison*. Vintage Books.
Foucault, M. (2002). *The archaeology of knowledge*. Routledge.
Foucault, M. (2005). *The order of things. An archaeology of the human sciences*. Routledge.
Foucault, M. (2010). *The government of self and others. Lectures at the Collège de France 1982–1983* (F. Gros, Ed.). Palgrave Macmillan.
Foucault, M. (2011). *The courage of truth: The government of self and others II. Lectures at the Collège de France 1983–1984* (F. Gros, Ed.). https://doi.org/10.1057/9780230309104
Gillies, D. (2013). *Educational leadership and Michel Foucault*. Routledge.
Gomart, E., & Hennion, A. (1999). A sociology of attachment: Music amateurs, drug users. *The Sociological Review, 47*(1_suppl), 220–247. https://doi.org/10.1111/j.1467-954x.1999.tb03490.x
Grimaldi, E., & Barzanò, G. (2014). Making sense of the educational present: Problematising the 'merit turn' in the Italian eduscape. *European Educational Research Journal, 13*(1), 26–46. https://doi.org/10.2304/eerj.2014.13.1.26
Grimaldi, E., Landri, P., & Serpieri, R. (2016). NPM and the reculturing of the Italian education system. The making of new fields of visibility. In H. M. Gunter, E. Grimaldi, D. Hall, & R. Serpieri (Eds.), *New public management and the reform of education. European lessons for policy and practice*. Routledge.
Gunther, H. M., Grimaldi, E., Hall, D., & Serpieri, R. (Eds.). (2016). *New public management and the reform of education*. Routledge.
Hennion, A. (2007). Those things that hold us together: Taste and sociology. https://doi.org/10.1177/1749975507073923
Hennion, A. (2017). Attachments, you say? ... How a concept collectively emerges in one research group. *Journal of Cultural Economy, 10*(1), 112–121. https://doi.org/10.1080/17530350.2016.1260629
Landri, P. (2009). A temporary eclipse of bureaucracy. The circulation of school autonomy in Italy. *Italian Journal of Sociology of Education, 1*(3), 76–93.
Landri, P., & Serpieri, R. (Eds.). (2004). *Il Ministero Virtuale. La pubblica istruzione online*. Liguori.
Latour, B. (1984). *Les Microbes: guerre et paix, suivi de Irréductions*. LaDécouverte.
Latour, B. (1999a). Factures/fractures: From the concept of network to the concept of attachment. *Res, 36*, 20–31.
Latour, B. (1999b). On recalling ANT. In J. Law & J. Hassard (Eds.), *Actor-network theory and after* (pp. 15–25). Blackwell Publishers Ltd.

Latour, B. (2004). How to talk about the body? The normative dimension of science studies. *Body & Society, 10*(2–3), 205–229. https://doi.org/10.1177/1357034X04042943

Law, J. (1994). *Organizing modernity. Social ordering and social theory.* Blackwell Publishers Ltd.

Law, J. (1998). After ANT: Complexity, naming and topology. *The Sociological Review, 46*(S), 1–14. https://doi.org/10.1111/1467-954X.46.s.1

Law, J., & Hassard, J. (Eds.). (1999). *Actor-network theory and after.* Blackwell Publishers Ltd.

Nicolini, D. (2010). Zooming in and out: Studying practices by switching theoretical lenses and trailing connections. *Organization Studies, 30*(12), 1391–1418. https://doi.org/10.1177/0170840609349875

Peters, M. A., & Taglietti, D. (2019). Deleuze's rhizomatic analysis of Foucault: Resources for a new sociology? *Educational Philosophy and Theory, 51*(12), 1187–1199. https://doi.org/10.1080/00131857.2018.1551831

Revel, J. (2016). Between politics and ethics: The question of subjectivation. In L. Cremonesi, O. Irrera, D. Lorenzini, & M. Tazzioli (Eds.), *Foucault and the making of subjects* (pp. 163–174). Rowman & Littlefield.

Serpieri, R. (2009). A 'war' of discourses. The formation of educational headship in Italy. *Italian Journal of Sociology of Education, 1,* 122–142.

Souto-Otero, M., & Beneito-Montagut, R. (2016). From governing through data to governmentality through data: Artefacts, strategies and the digital turn. *European Educational Research Journal, 15*(1), 14–33. https://doi.org/10.1177/1474904115617768

Taglietti, D. (2016). An archaeological analysis of the last Italian education reform policy. *Italian Journal of Sociology of Education, 8*(3), 195–221.

Taglietti, D., Grimaldi, E., & Serpieri, R. (2018). The good school/the bad headteacher: Neo-managerialism and the re-making of the headteacher. In E. Samier & P. Milley (Eds.), *International perspectives on maladministration in education: Theories, research, and critiques.* Routledge.

Zuboff, S. (2019). *The age of surveillance capitalism: The fight for a human future at the new frontier of power.* Public Affairs-Hachette Book Group.

CHAPTER 8

How Do Portuguese Principals Deal with Competing Demands? Issues of Bureaucracy, Performativity and Democracy

Maria Assunção Flores and Fernando Ilídio Ferreira

Abstract

This chapter reports on findings from a broader piece of research focusing on the views and experiences of leadership from the point of view of school principals and teachers. Data were collected through focus group and interviews. Findings point to the increased complexity of the principals' role, ambiguity in the use of the terms principal and administration team and the need of the school principals to deal with competing demands situated in different logics around issues of performativity, bureaucracy and democracy. Implications of the findings are discussed.

Keywords

school leadership – school management – principals – context

1   Introduction

Research literature on school leadership has expanded over the last decades. However, little agreement exists about how leadership is defined. This expansion can be positive, yet critical surveillance is needed in the face of the existing quantity, diversity and competing school leadership perspectives. Educational leadership has been converted into a seductive and fashionable topic, much of the times associated with the business world. As Peck and Reitzug (2012) state, business management concepts became school leadership fashion.

In turn, Alvesson and Spicer (2012, p. 369) describe what they consider to be a "conceptual confusion and endemic vagueness" which marks the field. The dominant portion of leadership theories and research is mostly concerned with relationships between leaders and their immediate followers or with supervisory behaviors (Hunt & Dodge, 2000). Collinson (2018, p. 261) identifies three main paradigms in the leadership field. Firstly, heroic approaches focus on effective leaders' qualities and practices (e.g. trait, style, contingency, path-goal, charisma, trust, emotional intelligence, etc.) and they tend to assume that the interests of leaders and followers automatically coalesce. Secondly, post-heroic perspectives emphasize the relational and collective dynamics (e.g. distributed, shared, collaborative) as well as the importance of followers, cultures, and contexts. Thirdly, critical leadership studies draw on dialectical perspectives to examine asymmetrical power relations in leadership dynamics, emphasizing that the leaders have considerable power. However, power can be paradoxical and contradictory, and the dialectics of power entails the need to reconsider leader-follower relations.

Also, there is a necessity to take into account the contextual, relational, ethical and political dimensions of school leadership. To a great extent, contextual and relational dimensions of school leadership have developed in the light of complexity theory (Eacott, 2018, 2019). Hallinger (2018) argues that most reviews of research on educational leadership published over the past five decades have treated context as a 'given' and demonstrated a tendency to 'average' findings drawn from diverse studies. These contextual factors appear highly relevant when practitioners outside economically developed, Anglo-American countries consider the applicability of these research findings. Hallinger (2018) emphasizes the importance of making the context features explicit, suggesting the need to broaden the lens of context for leadership to include economic, political and socio-cultural contexts. For example, there are affinities within the so-called Mediterranean countries in regard to the financial and social crises over the last decade related to Troika[1] intervention and the experience of austerity, especially in Portugal and Greece (Flores & Ferreira, 2016; Argyropoulou, 2018). These and other authors have called attention to the different geographies of the financial crisis and austerity (Kitson, Martin, & Tyler, 2011; Martin, 2011) and to the ideological gap between Troika policies and those embedded in peripheral countries (Clifton, Diaz-Fuentes, & Gómez, 2018).

The ways in which school leadership enacts policies in context have also been the focus of attention in existing literature. As Mango states, principals are "situated precisely at the accountability nexus between education policy and practice" (Mango, 2013, p. 179). In this regard, Vekeman, Devos, and Tuytens (2015, p. 130) argue that "the principal's agenda of policy implementation may be either consistent or conflictual with the expectations of teachers". In a similar vein, Tuytens and Devos (2010) concluded that the structure a principal provides, along with the trust teachers have in their principal, is of central importance to teachers' perceptions of the policy's practicality.

Leadership is essentially a relational phenomenon, as Branson and Marra (2019) also state. It emerges from practices and interactions among people throughout the organization. However, they underline a more research-informed practical understanding of relational leadership practice. They argue that assertions concerning the relevance of context to understanding leadership practice have implications for research. In this regard a relevant warning is made by Shamir (2011): "Leadership Takes time", referring to the necessity of taking time seriously in leadership research. It implies dismantling contemporary deficit thinking, valuing educational thought and practice (Valencia, 2010). This research-based leadership perspective suggests a "leadership of emergence" (Lichtenstein & Plowman, 2009) and a conception of leadership as "bricolage" (Jenlink, 2001, 2006). For example, the view of the school leader as bricoleur draws attention to the complex and problematic nature of schools in which the leader conducts his or her practice (Jenlink, 2001, 2006). As Jenking (2006) states, for the bricoleur, there is not a one-best way or means, but multiple perspectives and possibilities of solving problems and making decisions. The bricoleur's work is to balance the technical demands of daily life in the school with intellectual needs of the students and staff, fostering an academic environment for learning as well as a democratic community for students, practitioners, and parents. The result of the bricoleur's methods of practice is a bricolage (Denzin & Lincoln, 2000), a construction that arises from the reflexive interactions of different types of knowledge, mediating artifacts, and methods in relation to the social contexts, cultural patterns, and social actions and activities that comprise the daily events of the school.

Empirical studies point to the influence of school leadership in fostering teacher learning and development (Flores, 2004) as well as the key role and the complexity of school leadership in implementing policy initiatives by making sense of them (Flores, 2010, 2018; Tuytens & Devos, 2010, 2011). In a study looking at emerging forms of school leadership drawn from a literature review and accounts of practice based on research conducted in 20 schools, Chapman, Ainscow, Bragg, Gunter, Hull, Mongon, Muijs, and West (2009) argue that existing literature is more comprehensive in some areas than in others, and it tends to be descriptive rather than analytic and has many gaps. In addition, they found that school leaders have recognized that they face increased challenges and complexity within the system. Other research has shown how school leaders enact policies in context managing tensions and balancing conflicting goals (Flores & Derrington, 2017) as well as the interplay of the relationships between school context, principal leadership and mediating variables in leadership for learning (Paletta, Alivernini, & Manganelli, 2017).

This chapter looks at how principals enact policies in schools in the Portuguese context. It focuses on how they deal with competing demands within a centralized and bureaucratic educational system along with the revolutionary imaginary of democracy and freedom as generated by the Carnation

Revolution and the performativity and accountability pressures associated with more recent policies and the emergence of the concept of leadership.

2 The Portuguese Context

2.1 *Portugal in the Context of the Peripheral Countries*

The terms "Core and Peripheral countries" are used in the sense they were defined in the world-systems theory proposed by Wallerstein (2002): the Eurozone as a world system, the core as Germany and to a larger extent the 6 founding members of the EC, and as the peripheral countries the PIGS. The derogatory term 'PIGS', derived from the initial letters of the countries of the Southern European countries of Portugal, Italy, Greece and Spain, is embedded in negative representations of the period during which the South of Europe had been the undemocratic part of Europe, with Spain, Portugal and Greece having a dictatorship until the seventies; the underdeveloped part of Europe, with a poor economy; and culturally "slow people", with prejudices about the siesta, laziness, etc. (Van Vossole, 2014, 2016).[2] Particularities of these South European countries include, apart from the experience of dictatorship, the centralized tradition of the State and Public Administration; the subordination to the political and economic neoliberal pressures specially since the 1980's; the ambiguity of dealing with competing issues such as bureaucracy, performativity and democracy. These affinities were not only visible with the Great Recession of 2008. In capitalist countries manpower planning became widespread in the 1960s and the pioneering project was the Mediterranean Regional Project (MRP), launched in 1961, by the OECD for the six Mediterranean countries (Portugal, Spain, Italy, Greece, Yugoslavia and Turkey) to produce educational plans with a common conceptual work (OECD, 1965, 1966).

The derogatory and stereotyping term 'PIGS' (Capucha et al., 2014) already existed in the 1980s and 1990s (Lopreite, 2011), but its derogatory nature remerged with more intensity in the context of the 2008 financial crisis, that has also affected Ireland. In the acronym, the letter 'I' has become to represent Ireland or Italy. Before the crisis in the last decade, it has been mainly used in economics and finance, but after 2008 the term became popular, mainly after its first use in the *Financial Times* in 2008 in an article about the economic situation in Southern Europe entitled 'Pigs in muck',[3] appearing thereafter in publications such as *Newsweek* and *The Economist*.[4] Van Vossole's (2014, 2016) explores the racist framing of the peripheral member states of the European Union, the PIGS (Portugal, Ireland (and/or Italy), Greece and Spain) and demonstrates a strong connection between the processes of racialization and depoliticization, as well as the return of colonial dynamics in the Eurozone.

The financial crisis was perceived as "an 'opportunity' grasped by core members of the Eurozone – led by Germany – to impose neoliberal policies onto ailing members in the periphery, especially, onto South Europe" (Clifton, Diaz-Fuentes, & Gómez, 2018, p. 5). The end objective, according to Streeck (2016), was to compel countries that deviated from "acceptable" models of political economy, such as the "Mediterranean" variants, to be aligned with the neoliberal model required in the emerging "European Consolidation State". As Germany and other Northern countries gained the upper hand, Streeck (2016) argues they used the crisis as an opportunity to impose fiscal consolidation onto the rest of Eurozone members, shaping the future direction of the euro to their interests. Between 2010 and 2018, the Troika intervened six times, including one intervention each in Ireland, Portugal and Cyprus, and three in Greece, demonstrating that the crisis and austerity have led to human consequences much more severe in some countries and regions than others (Donald et al., 2014; Flores & Ferreira, 2016; Argyropoulou, 2018; Clifton, Diaz-Fuentes, & Gómez, 2018). Many European countries in the "core" north have overcome relatively well the crisis while others, mainly in the periphery, continue to face long term problems such as high levels on unemployment, cuts in the public sector, etc. (Kitson et al., 2011; Cuadrado-Roura et al., 2016).

As such, leadership studies have predominantly mirrored the "core" north context and neglected or considered Mediterranean countries as peripheral under the global and European Union managerial trends. The economic, financial and business lexicon, as well as that of the New Public Management, has invaded the educational field, thus emphasizing a representation of leadership associated with productivity and performativity – the one best way – and overlooking its historical, political and sociocultural contextual dimensions.

2.2   *The Emergence of the Leadership Concept*

In Portugal, the notion of leadership was introduced in the publication of the Decree-Law No. 75 in 2008 which stipulates a new school governance. In this framework it is stated that the principal is "the face" and the "first responsible" for the school. Before 2008, democratic school management was the mainstream notion. The terms used before the red Carnation revolution (1974) such as rector and school director/principal were replaced by the word "president" (president of a collegial body called as directive or executive council). The president used to be a teacher elected amongst his/her peers (see Decree-Law No. 115-A/98, 4th May).

Within the new legislative text issued in 2008, the school principal is no longer elected. He/she is appointed by the General Council of the school according to a recruitment process. He/she should have adequate qualifications for the role, including either training or experience in school administration and management. The same framework stipulates a new school governance (the principal), the aim of which is to "reinforce leadership at school". Notions such as "strong leadership" and "effective leadership" as well as the innocuous term of "good leadership" are advocated in the Decree-Law No. 75/2008. In addition, leadership is seen as mere implementation, in so far as it defines the "authority of the principal" as a way to "locally execute policy initiatives issued by the central government". This shift is based on the argument that schools need effective leadership, but it also reveals a conception of leadership that moves away from the collegiality and democracy dimensions that marked the previous models of school management in which the election amongst peers was a central element.

This new scenario has generated great controversy and debate involving policy makers, teachers' unions, academics and teachers. According to the new legislation, the principal is given more power in order to reinforce school leadership and to enhance effectiveness, but it also represents more responsibility. He/she simultaneously assumes the presidency of the Pedagogical Council and designates the coordinators of the curriculum departments which are the main pedagogical coordinating and supervising structures at school (in the previous legislation, the coordinators of the curriculum department were elected amongst teachers who integrated each department).

As such, the lexicon typical of a centralized and bureaucratic administration was expanded to include the emerging managerialistic lexicon such as efficacy, efficiency, goals and objectives, measurable and quantifiable results, standards to assess quality, competitiveness, performance, excellence, etc. Managerialism has been growing in the educational discourse along with its attractive lexicon which became greatly valued and used in schools, particularly by the principals, an example of which may be seen in the existence of "merit places" which have been institutionalized in many Portuguese schools clearly linked to the attractiveness of the discourse of excellence.

2.3   *A Scarcity of Research on School Leadership in Portugal*
While research on school administration and management has expanded and consolidated in the Portuguese context, empirical studies on leadership are rather scarce. To the best of our knowledge, few researchers have focused on school leadership. Existing empirical work has focused on a functionalist approach within a normative and prescriptive logic. Critical studies are scarce. Research

has focused on the ways in which school principals provide information, ideas, insights, strategies and instruments for school improvement purposes, including the bureaucratic, financial and resources management, the creation of a safe and healthy working environment; the vision and mission of the school, successful learning, etc.

Existing literature has addressed the problems they encounter in their job and the strategies they use to face them. Drawing on a survey, Silva (2017) looked at principals' preparation (n = 543) to their role in schools as well as the problems they face and their views on their professionalization. Principals state that they have an adequate preparation in terms of understanding of the community culture, sense of credibility on the part of the local community, promotion of positive relationships, partnership development, work and rapport with the school General Council, self-confidence as a leader and improvement of the teaching-learning process. Findings also show a higher level of preparation in regard to aspects related to the local domain. As for the problems they encounter, they are associated with managing bureaucracy, work and personal life balance, time management, equipment purchase, balance between system imperatives and local needs, financial management and staff recruitment. The author also found that the majority of the principals have vast experience in school management and specific training in the field. In general, they consider their training to be useful and are in support for the professionalization of their position.

Also, Pessoa (2017), in her study on school leadership from the perspective of principals, senior leadership teams and teachers, point to the school principal as being accountable for the entire school community, building on the core values of leadership, maintaining a safe and healthy working environment, and developing a culture of successful learning. The participants also value the following key dimensions as important for the position of school principal: strategic orientation, vision and mission; teaching and learning process; interpersonal relations and development; organization and resource management; accountability and community relations and contexts.

A recent study by Espuny et al. (2020) focusing on principals' problems identified political and social pressures on them to increase student achievement without the necessary support from the part of the educational authorities and the community. Furthermore, the same study found that, amongst others, school principals face a number of problems related to the creation and development of clusters of schools,[5] the overdependence on the educational authorities, the lack of relevant training and support and bureaucracy.

Drawing on a wider research project and adopting a more interpretative approach to leadership practice, Flores and Ferreira (2019) looked at principals, teachers and pupils understanding of leadership and found that a number of tensions emerged, particularly in regard to the principals' need to deal with contradictory job demands, namely the demands of increasing pupil achievement and with the need to actively invest in initiatives for social support to families and children. The same authors conclude that leadership for learning is not embedded in the school principals' representation of their role. In addition, the same study found that school principals had to cope with the traditional and persistent bureaucratic centralism and with the new demands of managerialism, accountability and performativity.

In light of critical perspectives, it is important to look at how school principals have been dealing with competing forces and pressures over the last decade, namely bureaucracy, democracy and performativity, taking into account the historical and cultural features of the Portuguese context.

3 Methods

This chapter presents findings arising from a wider 3-year project funded by Fundação para a Ciência e a Tecnologia (National Foundation for Science and Technology) (PTDC/CPE-CED/112164/2009) focusing on leadership and school culture. It addresses the following research questions:
1. How do principals and teachers perceive school leadership role in a context of school reform?
2. How do school principals enact policies in context?

3.1 Data Collection and Analysis

The research followed a mixed-method design in a sequential way. It included three phases of data collection which took place between 2012 and 2014. In the first phase, a national survey was conducted with 2702 teachers. A second phase of data collection was then carried out using semi-structured interviews with principals in 11 schools located in different regions of the country and focus groups with 99 teachers and 108 students. Finally, the phase III comprised a professional development program carried out in 5 schools located in northern Portugal, in which 66 teachers participated. In this chapter data arising from the semi-structured interviews with the principals and focus groups with the teachers will be reported.

In total, 22 focus group were conducted. Each focus group comprised 3 to 7 participants. Teachers participating in the focus groups were recruited by the principal in each of the 11 participating schools. A diversity set of criteria was used to select the participants such as years of experience, gender, level of teaching, roles performed at school, subject taught, etc. The focus group protocol included questions related to perceptions of school culture and leadership, changes in teachers' work, and issues related to being a teacher and to teaching as a profession. The focus groups were conducted in each of the schools by at least two researchers participating in the wider research project. The semi-structured interviews with the principals also focused on their views on school culture and leadership, and teachers' work.

Data collected from the interviews and focus groups were analyzed in two phases: an analysis of data gathered in each interview and focus group; a second phase was then carried out according to a comparative or horizontal analysis (Miles & Huberman, 1994). In the second phase, common patterns as well as differences were examined.

3.2 Participants

The majority of the teachers participating in the focus groups were female (76.8%) with 31.3% aged between 51 and 60 years old and 27.3% between 41 and 50 years old. The participating teachers came from all levels of teaching, from pre-school to secondary school.[6] In regard to their experience as teachers, 36.4% had between 21 and 30 years of service, 26.3% between 31 and 40, and 22.2% between 11 and 20 years of experience. More than 50.0% of them had more than 10 years of experience in the current school.

In general, the age of the teachers participating in the survey and in the focus groups is similar to the official statistics described in the "General profile of the teachers" in Portugal, published by the Ministry of Education. According to the last official statistics, 48.4% of the teachers in Portugal are 50 years or older and only 0.4% are 30 years of age or younger, figures that apply to the public sector (DGEEC, 2018). According to the recent TALIS report (OECD, 2019), the average teacher is 44 years old, but in Portugal is 49 years of age. The same report states that there was a "dramatic change" since TALIS 2013. In other words, there was a significant increase of teachers aged 50 or above in Portugal from 28.0% in TALIS 2013 to 47.0% in TALIS 2018.

Of the 11 principals, 6 were female and they came from all sectors of education, including large clusters of schools (from pre-school to secondary schools) (7); 4 worked in the secondary school sector only. They had between 18 and 32 years of experience as teachers and principals. Two principals had more than 20 years of experience in their current school.

According TALIS 2018 (OECD, 2019), Portuguese principals are, on average, 54 years old, which is higher than the average age of principals across the OECD (52 years old). Furthermore, 23.0% of principals in Portugal are aged 60 and above, compared to 20.0% on average across the OECD countries. In addition,

43.2% are female teachers whereas female teachers represent 73.7% of the teaching workforce.

School principals participating in the study reported in this chapter have a great deal of experience both as teachers and as members of management, coordination and administration structures at school. Most of them act as school principals for several years and they had been Presidents of the Executive Council prior to 2008 when the new legislative text introducing the figure of the principal was issued. Most of them have done training in school management and organization, educational administration, educational policy and pedagogical supervision, some of them at a master and PhD level.

4 Findings

4.1 *The Experience of Leadership: Principals and Teachers' Views*

The notion of "democratic management of schools" emerged after the Carnation revolution. It was, in fact, included in the Constitution of the Portuguese Republic in 1976 and it remains currently: "Teachers and students have the right to participate in the democratic management of schools" (art. 77, n. 1). Since then the notion of democratic management of schools has been used a lot at a policy level and at the level of school administration, but it has been gradually away from political power discourses, educational policies and legislative texts. As such, it is mainly in the spontaneous discourse of the teachers and school principals that this concept remains, in an explicit or implicit way, as part of their imaginary, or as a result of the naturalization process of the concept.

As the school principals are older than 50 years of age, most of them were students or youth, when the Carnation revolution took place (1974), and, thus, they had a connection to this historical event. However, as the study reported in this chapter focused on leadership, in the interviews and focus groups the participants, both teachers and principals, used the term democratic leadership.

> My goal is that my leadership is democratic … sometimes you have to be more directive, sometimes you can be more permissive in the sense of being more tolerant and trying to understand the context in which things happen. (Principal)

> She [the school principal] does not do anything in an authoritarian way, I would say, but she operates in a democratic way. She uses to say "so, what do you think? Is it okay?" (Teacher)

> I think his leadership is a democratic one. Although most of the decisions are part of the principals' role, in this school we are heard and consulted both at the department level and at the level of the subject group. (Teacher)

> I think that there is a difference between being a boss and being a leader. The boss is the one who makes decisions and makes orders and people obey. This vision does not exist here. Here you find a democratic vision. The principal knows how to make orders but she also does things when needed. (Teacher)

Ideas such as freedom and participation also emerged from the participants' accounts. They are related to a great extent to an open attitude from the part of the principal as he/she allows the freedom of choice and initiative in forming teams instead of imposition.

> We look at our colleague (principal) as someone who does not say: "let's do this activity. You have to do it". She does not impose it on you. It is the way she puts it: "It would be interesting if we could do this". (Teacher)

> This year there was the possibility from the part of teachers to choose who they wanted to work with. Basically all teams were composed according to the participants' views. They were done according to the initiative and participation of people who are collaborating in a very positive way in the activities and in team work. It was interesting that the principal had this kind of open attitude instead of imposition. (Teacher)

It is important to note that the legislative texts issued after 25 April 1974 stipulated the so-called directive council and later executive council as collegial bodies elected by the teachers. This model was in place until 2008. Whilst in the previous management models, a collegial body elected by the teachers in each school run the school, after the publication of Decree-Law No. 75/2008, the principal became the head of the school. He/she is no longer elected but is appointed by the General Council and he/she has the power to appoint the teachers to the various roles and functions at the school, namely the assistant principal, the support staff/teachers for the leadership team, coordinators of departments and school coordinators as well as the tutors for each group of pupils.

In the interviews teachers do not mention the notions of effective and strong leadership as it is advocated in the legislative text issued in 2008. On the contrary, in various moments, the school principal was described as a colleague, within a perspective of collegiality that was not abolished with the institutionalization by decree of a one-person structure, i.e., the school principal. Even when the term principal is used, it is not necessarily in the perspective of one-person structure or even less as the same as the leader of the school. From a legal point of view, the school principal is a one-person structure, but it seems that this understanding was not part of the representations and practices of the teachers when this study took place. The idea of a team – the administration team – is more emphasized. In other words, there is ambiguity in the use of the terms principal and administration team. Both terms are recurring in teachers' accounts but in an unconscious way. The term principal is used when teachers want to refer to the person in concrete whereas administration team points to the collegial body responsible for the running of the school (with a president and vice-presidents) that no longer exists in the current legislative text but remains present in teachers' subjectivities as it corresponds to a reality that was familiar to them for many years.

> The principal knows how to set up the priorities and how to put them into practice, but he does not make decisions without listening to his team. He tries to articulate the philosophy of the project and the administration team. I think it is good to live and work in such an environment. It is about team work. (Teacher)

> We know that it is not the role of one person that makes the school work: what makes the school work is the 200 people who work here. I think that, above all, all of us are teachers and those who are part of the administration team are teachers as well. We make the school work as well as students, support staff and above all the teachers. (Teacher)

The teachers participating in the focus groups refer to the term "team" when they want to talk about those in leadership roles, whether in the school administration or the school coordinators or heads of department.

> The school coordinator has a pivotal role in creating a team spirit. Today schools are living a very tough reality and the coordinator has to handle everything. He has to be the facilitator and has to help teachers to deal with the pressure imposed on them. We need to feel that he is there for us. (Teacher)

One of the most positive aspects related to the principal is the willingness to listen to people and the open attitude, particularly in relation to the teachers:

HOW DO PORTUGUESE PRINCIPALS DEAL WITH COMPETING DEMANDS? 147

> I think he has an open attitude and he communicates well. He is in the school all day, and he isn't locked in his office. He listens to his colleagues. (Teacher)

> She is a person who knows how to listen to people and what to do; she is directive but not authoritarian; she gives instructions but she doesn't impose them. (Teacher)

Teachers' discourses are full of adjectives pointing to issues of openness and communication when they talk about their principals. The following quotation illustrates this idea as one teacher spoke of "being able to listen" as a personal quality and ability revealed in a conversation and as strategy to persuade people to adhere to her vision and "turn things to her advantage":

> She listens to us and then she turns things to her advantage. When we look back, we can see it was worth it, we can see how much we have achieved. (Teacher)

In turn, the principals also highlight the importance of "listening" as a key dimension of their role, as it is part of the solution for a given problem:

> I guess listening is a key element because the ability to listen is part of the solution for the problems. (Principal)

A similar view is held by the participating teachers who claim that they are "consulted" whenever a decision is to be made or whenever their view is important to solve a given situation or problem. Being heard is described by the teachers as a key element in their motivation and encouragement to carry out their job:

> Encouragement exists because you feel you are heard; your views are taken into account! (Teacher)

In face of multiple, and in a way contradictory demands, the principals use a number of strategies in order to deal with them: being in tune with the school, being empathetic, a focus on the pupils and "being aware of what you ask from each one of the staff" (Principal):

> It is about being in tune with the school. This does not mean that you agree with what people think, because I can stand for my point of view

by myself. But it is about being in tune with the school, being empathetic, I mean it is about mutual support. (Principal)

For me the key element is the pupils. It is because of them that you are here, the rest is a number of strategies that you develop to get there. (Principal)

4.2 Leadership and the Enactment of the Policy Initiatives in Context

One of the challenges of the Portuguese principals was associated with the bulk of reforms, particularly over the last fifteen years. Teacher and school evaluation are two examples that are recurrent in the discourse of the participants. For instance, school evaluation, initiated in 2006–2007, is developed by the General Inspection of Education. The "frame of reference for external evaluation of schools" entails and is seen by the schools as an act of control which culminates in the dissemination of a ranking of schools in the country. Although the external model of school evaluation demands and even promotes the elaboration of a self-evaluation scheme from the part of the schools, it entails a centralized control and accountability mechanism which at the same time weakens the contextualized meaning of autonomy and school leadership. It is, therefore, seemingly contradictory the political call for leadership – although its meaning is understood as a managerialistic, instrumental, non-participatory and non-empowered leadership – and the growing emphasis on programs and initiatives from the Central Administration to which schools respond often as something mandatory. The three domains according to which schools are evaluated are: results; development of the educational service: and leadership and management. Leadership became a key element. A look at the principal indicators related to the category "leadership and management" reveals that aspects associated with administrative and pedagogical management, as well as human resources, are prevalent leaving behind elements related to pupils and their well-being and learning.

The school principals participating in the study refer to these competing demands in their job. On the one hand, they have to guarantee the democratic and inclusive nature of the school – a school for everybody with equal opportunities – and, on the other hand, they have to deal with pressures that point, in recent years, to the re-emergence of a meritocratic, elitist school based on the transposition to the school setting of the merit and excellence ideology, etc.

Being a school principal nowadays is a complex mission as you need to harmonize contradictory demands. (Principal)

The competition in relation to school achievement ... now there is such scenario in education, I mean, rankings, good schools and bad schools. And this has something perverse. But the good thing about our school is that it is an inclusive school. It takes into account the needs and specific features of each person and it responds in a differentiated way to each person. (Principal)

One of my biggest concerns is to reconcile the situation of mass schooling and inclusion on the one hand and results and achievement on the other hand. Either we slow down the elitism and thus we could select the students ... or the so-called inclusion policy does not allow us to be a reference school in terms of results. (Principal)

Aware of the multiple and contradictory demands, the school principals think and develop their work trying to harmonize different logics: (i) a logic of managerialism with issues of effectiveness, efficacy, optimization, etc.; (ii) a logic emphasizing a pedagogic dimension aimed at promoting learning and improvement of school results; and (iii) a logic with a social and community dimension through the reinforcement of the link between school and its environment (institutions, services, enterprises, etc.).

There was something that I included in my leadership project. Basically there were three very simple aspects. First, the teaching and learning process which has to do with the educational success, improvement of school results, decreasing of the number of students who fail or leave school; the second aspect has to do with the organizational dimension, i.e., the running of the school, in terms of effectiveness and efficacy, reducing costs and losses, and this is related to the restructuring of the services in order to make them operate better. The third dimension has to do with the connection between the school and the community, with the environment, in order to foster the link with the enterprises, and institutions (Principal).

Issues such as involvement and participation were also at the forefront of the principals' accounts when they talked about their leadership. Shared leadership and mobilizing people were recurring elements.

I exert leadership always having in mind the involvement and participation of people and decentralizing as much as possible as in my view power has to be shared. Power cannot be in the hands of one sole person. (Principal)

> I guess it is a participatory leadership because it draws on the conversation with all of the stakeholders. I ask teachers to participate in projects, I look at their abilities and qualifications and I try to get the best of them, the best they can do for the school. (Principal)

> In fact, there is a shared leadership in this school. Our principal has an open attitude; she leaves the decisions in our hands. She doesn't want to make all the decisions. All big decisions are shared with middle leadership. (Teacher)

> Leadership is something that needs to be built. It is something that is built step by step. (Teacher)

In the interviews both teachers and principals spoke of leading by the example, through the involvement in the school work and the visibility in the school. At the same time, the participants refer to the importance of creating an ethos of collaboration and a cohesive team, particularly when the complex merging of schools took place (then becoming large clusters of schools).

> The principal has been trying to unifying people because the formation of the cluster was complex, very complex. It has been very tiring and he has been trying to avoid conflicts between those who belonged to this school and the teachers who belonged to the other school. There were two independent schools, there was not much connection between them. (Teacher)

> It is a very tough process to unite three schools that are completely different. You need a great profile, a humanistic profile in order to manage that and the principal has done a great job in this regard. (Principal)

There are a number of constraints and difficulties identified by the principals related to the school, to the teachers and to their own role. Most of them are associated with normativity, regulations and the number of bureaucratic mechanisms that asphyxiate schools, teachers' work and the action of principals.

> Over the last few years the school has become more difficult to manage because the principal is asked to respond to a number of queries from the part of the deconcentrated and centralized services of Central Administration. It is overwhelming and all this on top of the day-to-day management of the school. (Principal)

> Bureaucracy is too much, that is why I try to do meetings the least possible. People do deserve respect because we need to prioritize their pedagogical work. (Principal)

As Sergiovanni (2004) argues, if school improvement is to be achieved, "pedagogical leadership" is the most effective alternative to bureaucratic leadership. The participating principals noted the difficulties in dealing with all the administrative and bureaucratic demands of their job and their willingness to focus on pedagogical matters:

> I waste much of my time in administrative tasks. My main role is related to the Pedagogical Council. It is where I feel my job is useful and I feel good about it. The Pedagogical Council is the heart of the school and it is where you make the great decisions, you reorganize things, you define strategies. (Principal)

However, educational policy and reforms, and mainly isolated legislative initiatives, affect negatively the life of schools as they remove time and space for the exercise of pedagogical leadership and tend to create an illusion around change. As one principal puts it, it is about "a game of pretending to change".

> In the current political moment, it is about a game of pretending to change, built on a very nice discourse, sometimes very pleasant, everybody accepts that and the media thinks that everything is good. (Principal)

> There is a lot of bureaucracy, too much bureaucracy actually. Then you are asked to do things that you don't believe. You have to do stuff on the online platforms, to fill in forms, surveys, etc. Sometimes it is a replication of you have already done. (Principal)

> You cannot image how much time I spend in front of my computer to respond to last minute things, things that are incredible and that you are asked to do overnight and some of them completely meaningless. (Principal)

> It is frustrating because people do reports about lots of things, and they do planning and so on ... and I think that this excessive paperwork is taking people's energy and they don't do practical stuff. (Principal)

> You feel overwhelmed by bureaucracy that takes away from you space for other tasks that demand reflection, proximity and discussion. (Principal)

> Teachers are tired, they are overwhelmed and tired of being treated like that, I mean not treated well. [...] there have been too many reforms, legislation and so on. [...] You start to understand a given decree-law or any other legislative text, and suddenly another one gets to the schools. This is unbelievable. Somebody needs to stop that. (Principal)

One issue that also emerged in the principals' accounts is trust. The trust that exists between school principals and teachers does not exist at the level of the relationships between the Ministry of Education and the schools. The principals regret that as they state that this trust is essential as a way to liberate the school from the bureaucratic burden of various mechanisms of centralized control.

> Trust. I think teachers feel that we trust them. [...] One of the things that people have here is that they have space for taking the initiative ... people feel that they can take risks and if anything goes wrong we are available here to accept failure ... people feel that if anything goes wrong, they have somebody to turn to. (Principal)

> Teachers have confidence in the principal, trust does not mean doing whatever, it doesn't mean that evaluation doesn't exist [...] but you need trust and I feel that the Ministry of Education doesn't have that. (Principal)

5   Discussion

From this study three main conclusions can be drawn. First, findings point to the increased complexity of the principals' role as a result of the bulk of reforms, particularly the formation of the clusters of schools. This implied the merging of schools that used to operate independently with implications for school culture, leadership and teachers' identities.

Ten years after the publication of the Decree-Law No. 115-A/98, the government has approved a new legal framework (Decree-Law No. 75/08) in which notions such as autonomy and leadership are prevalent. This new legislative text keeps that same designation of the previous legislative text – "regime of autonomy, administration and management" – but it is precisely around leadership (used for the second time within the traditional domain of school management[7]) that a great debate was held involving teachers, teacher unions, academics, amongst other political and social stakeholders. The aim of this legal framework is "to reinforce leadership at school", by creating "conditions for good leadership and effective leadership to exist" (Decree-Law No. 75/08). In the legislative text published in 2008, it is possible to identify some tensions which are also associated with the data arising from our study, namely between the discourse of decentralization and school autonomy and the managerial discourse of accountability: (i) it is necessary that there is in each school a face, a first responsible, having the necessary authority to develop the educational project of the school and execute locally the educational policy initiatives; (ii) this first responsible is held accountable and he/she has responsibilities for the provision of a public service of education and for the management of public resources made available to him/her (Decree-Law No. 75/2008). This emphasizes the authority of the principal to "execute" locally the initiatives of educational policy defined by central administration, which points to a conception of leadership as mere implementation, and not to a conception of leadership that incorporates the production of policies in and for the school, in the sense that Ball, Maguire, and Braun (2012) attribute to the concept of "policy enactment" in schools.

Secondly, even though the school principal represents a one-person structure responsible for the running of the school, the idea of a team – the administration team – emerged from the data. From a legal point of view, the school principal is a one-person structure, but it seems that this understanding was not part of the representations and practices of the teachers when the study took place. On the contrary, in various comments, the school principal was described as a colleague, in line with the notion of collegiality. Ambiguity in the use of the terms principal and administration team is identified as they are used in an unconscious way. The term principal is used when teachers talk about the person in concrete whereas administration team refers to the collegial body responsible for the running of the school (with a president and vice-presidents) that no longer exists in the legislative text published in 2008 but remains present in teachers' subjectivities as it corresponds to a reality that was familiar to them for many years. This is to be related to the notion of "democratic management of schools" from the very beginning of the democratic times in Portugal which is still visible in the spontaneous discourse of the teachers and school principals, in an explicit or implicit way, as part of their imaginary, or as a result of the naturalization process of the concept. Interestingly teachers' discourses do not point to notions of effective and strong leadership as it is advocated in the legislative text issued in 2008.

Thirdly, principals have to deal with competing demands that point to different logics in the midst of which they are caught. Issues of performativity, bureaucracy and democracy are at the forefront of their work and ways of operating. Thus, the political call for leadership present in the legislative text issued in 2008 seems not to be compatible with the growing emphasis on programs and initiatives from the Central Administration to which schools respond often as something that is mandatory. In fact, the principal is expected to "execute locally the educational policy initiatives", thus, pointing to a rather managerialistic, instrumental, non-participatory and non-empowered conception of leadership. As such, educational policy and reforms affect negatively the life of the principals as they remove time and space for the exercise of pedagogical leadership and tend to create an illusion around change and autonomy. On the one hand, principals have to guarantee the democratic and inclusive nature of the school – a school for everybody with equal opportunities – and, on the other hand, they have to handle pressures associated with the re-emergence of a meritocratic, elitist school based on the transposition to the school setting of the merit and excellence ideology, etc. Thus, principals have to respond to the competing demands of their job within different logics: (i) a logic of managerialism with issues of effectiveness, efficacy, optimization, etc.; (ii) a logic emphasizing a pedagogic dimension aimed at promoting learning and improvement of school results; and (iii) a logic with a social and community meaning through the reinforcement of the link between school and its environment (institutions, services, enterprises, etc.).

5.1 *The Relevance of Context to Understand Leadership*
Existing literature on leadership has not given much attention to the importance of context of the school. Although many leadership studies entailed contextual dimensions, the most frequent ones focus on the economic-financial feature of a given context. Only few focus specifically on the socio-historical and cultural dimension of a given region, country, community or school. Critical leadership studies point to a wide, diverse and heterogeneous array of perspectives that share a concern to critique the power relations and identity constructions through which leadership dynamics are frequently reproduced and rationalized and sometimes resisted and transformed (Collinson, 2011, 2018).

Whilst within the normative approaches to leadership, context is not seen as a key element, as they are characterized by their uniformed and universalized nature, in critical approaches contextual dimensions are key features both in terms of action and in terms of research on policy and practices of leadership, locally, nationally and globally (Marion & Uhl-Bien, 2001; Moos, 2013; Ylimaki & Uljens, 2017; Eacot, 2019).

However, the mainstream literature tends to adopt a functionalist perspective more oriented towards adaptation than towards social transformation.

School environment is frequently seen either as a source of resources (e.g. partnerships, stakeholders, value added) or in terms of deficit (e.g. low levels of schooling of the parents, social neighborhoods, school leavers, unemployment, poverty). In both cases, the principals tend to be seen as key actors to attract those resources and to compensate those handicaps. Although these are different approaches, they are equivalent when it comes to leadership. The emphasis is put on the qualities of effective leaders, on leadership styles and kinds of intelligence leaders possess to manage people, on their competencies to solve problems, on their resilience to deal with adverse circumstances, all of which are summarized in the famous triad "values, vision and mission" leading to the development of creative checklists and toolkits/ toolboxes. The school leadership literature widely disseminated by international agencies such as the OECD clearly assumes this functionalist perspective, by abundantly disseminating normative and prescriptive injunctions. These comprise, for example, case studies presented as good practices; a tool kit for principals, etc. (OECD, 2008a, 2008b). More recently, this organization published "The future of education and skills" under the motto "Education 2030 – the future we want" (OECD, 2018).

As Collinson (2011) argues, the emergence of a comparatively new approach to studying leadership, the "critical leadership studies", has contributed to problematize the concept and the analytical perspectives of school leadership. Critical studies have questioned and tried to overcome the hegemonic perspectives in the mainstream literature that tend both to underestimate the complexity of leadership dynamics and to take for granted that leaders are the people in charge who make decisions, and that followers are those who merely carry out orders from 'above' (Collinson, 2011).

The findings presented in this chapter have shown how issues of power and relationships have been addressed by some Portuguese principals, but also how the complex and competing demands they have to deal with are handled in a context marked by contradictory messages. These call for new understandings of leadership and a more thorough analysis of the factors that mediate and influence its enactment in context.

Notes

1 Constituted by the European Commission (EC), the European Central Bank (ECB) and the International Monetary Fund (IMF).
2 The idea that the Mediterranean constitutes a lazy culture exists since the moment of second modernity; the moment when the core of the world system and its ideological center moved from the Iberian Peninsula to North-western Europe (Santos, 2009).
3 *Financial Times*, 31 August 2008.

4   Juliane von Reppert-Bismarck, 'Why PIGS can't fly' (in 2015 the title was changed to 'Why Southern Europe's economies don't compete'), *Newsweek*, 28 June 2008; and 'Ten years on, beware a porcine plot', *The Economist*, 5 June 2008.
5   The creation of big clusters of schools corresponded to an imposed policy from the Ministry of Education and its consequent shutting down of almost all rural schools in the country. The majority of these clusters of schools (67%) have more than 1200 students and 15% of them more than 2500 students (CNE, 2017).
6   Portuguese students normally spend nine years in Basic Education, from year 1 to year 9 (pupils aged 6–15). Secondary education lasts for three years (16–18 years old).
7   The term leadership was used for the first time in the previous legislative text (Decree-Law No. 115-A/1998), although at that time it was referred to in an innocuous way in the introduction but was not developed in the main text.

References

Alvesson, M., & Spicer, A. (2011). *Metaphors we lead by: Understanding leadership in the real world*. Routledge.

Argyropoulou, E. (2018). International organizations of educational planning, government policies and school management and leadership. *China-USA Business Review, 17*(2), 53–63.

Ball, S. J. (2003). The teacher's soul and the terrors of performativity. *Journal of Education Policy, 18*(2), 215–22.

Ball, S. J. (2011). A new research agenda for educational leadership and policy. *Management in Education, 25*(2), 50–52.

Ball, S. J., Maguire, M., & Braun, A. (2012). *How schools do policy: Policy enactments in secondary schools*. Routledge.

Branson, C. M., & Marra, M. (2019). Leadership as a relational phenomenon: What this means in practice. *Research in Educational Administration & Leadership, 4*(1), 81–108.

Capucha, L. Estêvão, P., Calado, A., & Capucha, A. R. (2014). The role of stereotyping in public policy legitimation: The case of the PIGS label'. *Comparative Sociology, 13*(4), 482–502.

Castanheira, P., & Costa, J. A. (2015). A liderança na gestão das escolas: contributos de análise organizacional. *RBPAE, 31*(1), 13–44.

Castellani, B., & Hafferty, F. W. (2009). *Sociology and complexity science. A new field of inquiry*. Springer.

Chapman, C., Ainscow, M., Bragg, J., Gunter, H., Hull, J., Mongon, D., Muijs, D., & West, M. (2009). *Emerging patterns of school leadership: Current practice and future directions* (Project report). National College for School Leadership, Nottingham, UK.

Clifton, J, Diaz-Fuentes, D., & Gómez, A. L. (2018). The crisis as opportunity? On the role of the Troika in constructing the European consolidation state. *Cambridge Journal of Regions, Economy and Society, 11*(3), 587–608.

Collinson, D. L. (2011). Critical leadership studies. In A. Bryman, D. Collinson, K. Grint, B. Jackson, & M. Uhl-Bien (Eds.), *The Sage handbook of leadership* (pp. 181–194). Sage.

Collinson, D. L. (2018). Critical leadership studies. Exploring the dialectics of leadership. In R. E. Riggio (Ed.), *What's wrong with leadership? Improving leadership research and practice* (pp. 260–278). Routledge.

Crevani, L., Lindgren, M., & Packendorff, J. (2010). Leadership, not leaders: On the study of leadership as practices and interactions. *Scandinavian Journal of Management, 26*(1), 77–86.

Cuadrado-Roura, J. R., Martin, R., & Rodríguez-Pose, A. (2016). The economic crisis in Europe: Urban and regional consequences. *Cambridge Journal of Regions, Economy and Society, 9*(1), 3–11.

Denzin, N., & Lincoln, Y. (2000). The discipline and practice of qualitative research. In N. K. Denzin & Y. S. Lincoln (Eds.), *Handbook of qualitative research* (pp. 1–32). Sage.

Donald, B., Glasmeier, A., Gray, M., & Lobao, L. (2014). Austerity in the city: Economic crisis and urban service decline? *Cambridge Journal of Regions, Economy and Society, 7*(1), 3–15.

Eacott, S. (2018). *Beyond leadership: A relational approach to organizational theory in education*. Springer.

Eacott, S. (2019). Starting points for a relational approach to organizational theory: An overview. *Research in Educational Administration and Leadership, 4*(1), 16–45.

Espuny, M. T., Cunha, R. S., Cabral, I., & Matias Alves, J. (2020). Giving voice to problems faced by school leaders in Portugal. *School Leadership & Management. 40*(4), 352–372. doi:10.1080/13632434.2020.1719400

Fairhurst, G. T. (2007). *Discursive leadership*. Sage.

Flores, M. A. (2004). The impact of school culture and leadership on new teachers' learning in the workplace. *International Journal of Leadership in Education, 7*(4), 297–318.

Flores, M. A. (2010). Teacher performance appraisal in Portugal: The (im)possibilities of a contested model. *Mediterranean Journal of Educational Studies, 15*(1), 41–60.

Flores, M. A. (2018). Teacher evaluation in Portugal: Persisting challenges and perceived effects. *Teachers and Teaching Theory and Practice, 24*(3), 223–245.

Flores, M. A., & Derrington, M. L. (2017). School principals' views of teacher evaluation policy: Lessons learned from two empirical studies. *International Journal of Leadership in Education, 20*(4), 416–431.

Flores, M. A., & Ferreira, F. I. (2016). Education and child poverty in times of austerity in Portugal: Implications for teachers and teacher education. *Journal of Education for Teaching, 42*(4), 404–416.

Flores, M. A., & Ferreira, F. I. (2019). Leading learning in schools in challenging times: Findings from research in Portugal. In T. Townsend (Ed.), *Instructional leadership and leadership for learning in schools* (pp. 133–162). Palgrave Macmillan.

Giroux, H. (1988). *Teachers as intellectuals: Toward a critical pedagogy of learning*. Bergin & Garvey Publishers.

Grundy, S. (1993). Educational leadership as emancipatory praxis. In J. Blackmore & J. Kenway (Eds.), *Gender matters in educational administration and policy: A feminst introduction* (pp. 165–177). Falmer.

Hallinger, P. (2018). Bringing context out of the shadows of leadership. *Educational Management Administration & Leadership, 46*(1), 5–24.

Hunt, J., & Dodge, G. (2000). Leadership déjà vu all over again. *The Leadership Quarterly, 11*(4), 435–458.

Jenlink, P. M. (2001). Beyond the knowledge base controversy: Advancing the ideal of scholar-practitioner leadership. In T. J. Kowalski (Ed.), *21st Century challenges for educational administration* (pp. 65–88). The Scarecrow Press.

Jenlink, P. M. (2006). The school leader as bricoleur: Developing scholarly practitioners for our schools. *Education Leadership Review, 7*(2), 54–69.

Keddie, A. (2015). School autonomy, accountability and collaboration: A critical review. *Journal of Educational Administration and History, 47*(1), 1–17.

Kitson, M., Martin, R., & Tyler, P. (2011). The geographies of austerity. *Cambridge Journal of Regions, Economy and Society, 4*(3), 289–302.

Lichtenstein, B. B., & Plowman, D. A. (2009). The leadership of emergence: A complex systems leadership theory of emergence at successive organizational levels. *The Leadership Quarterly, 20*(4), 617–630.

Lima, L. C. (2014). A gestão democrática das escolas: Do autogoverno à ascensão de uma pós-democracia gestionária? *Educação, Sociedade Campinas, 35*(129), 1067–1083.

Lopreite, M. (2011). The Portugal situation during the financial crisis. *Advances in Management and Applied Economics, 1*(1), 111–124.

Mango, C. S. (2013). *Comparative perspectives on international school leadership*. Routledge.

Martin, R. (2011). The local geographies of the financial crisis: From the housing bubble to recession and beyond. *Journal of Economic Geography, 11*(4), 587–618.

Meira, M. V. F. (2017). *A Burocracia Electrónica: Um Estudo sobre as Plataformas Electrónicas na Administração Escolar* (Tese de Doutoramento em Ciências da Educação, especialidade de Organização e Administração Escolar). Universidade do Minho.

Miles, M. B., & Huberman, A. M. (1994). *Qualitative data analysis: An expanded sourcebook*. Sage.

Morin, E. (1992). The concept of system and the paradigm of complexity. In M. Maruyama (Ed.), *Context and complexity. Cultivating contextual understanding* (pp. 125–136). SpringerVerlag.

Neto-Mendes, A., Costa, J. A., & Ventura, A. (Eds.). (2011). A emergência do diretor da escola: questões políticas e organizacionais. In *Atas do VI Simpósio sobre Organização e Gestão Escolar*. Universidade de Aveiro.

Ntampoudi, I. (2014). The Eurozone crisis and the politics of blaming: The cases of Germany and Greece. *Political Perspectives, 8*(2(3), 1–20.

OECD. (1965). *Le Projet Régional Méditerranéen: Six pays en quête d'un plan. Récite d'une expérience.* Author.

OECD. (1966). *Le Projet Régional Méditerranéen – Portugal.* Author.

OECD. (2018). *The future of education and skills. Education 2030. The future we want.* Author.

OECD. (2008a). *Improving school leadership: Case studies on system leadership* (Vol. 2). Author.

OECD. (2008b). *Improving school leadership: The tool kit.* Author. www.oecd.library/org

OECD. (2019). *TALIS 2018 results: Teachers and school leaders as lifelong learners* (Vol. 1). Author.

OECD. (2020). *TALIS 2018 results: Teachers and school leaders as valued professionals* (Vol. II). Author.

Paletta, A., Alivernini, F., & Manganelli, S. (2017). Leadership for learning: The relationships between school context, principal leadership and mediating variables. *International Journal of Educational Management, 31*(2), 98–117.

Peck, C., & Reitzug, U. (2012). How existing business management concepts became school leadership fashion. *Educational Administration Quarterly, 48*(2), 347–381.

Pessoa, C. M. (2017). *Liderança na escola de hoje, competências essenciais à liderança do diretor de escola* (Doctoral dissertation). Universidade Lusófona de Humanidades e Tecnologias, Lisboa.

Portugal. (1976). *Constitution of the Portuguese Republic.*

Portugal. (1998). *Decree-Law n.º 115-A/98, 4 May, Diário da República n.º 102/1998, 1º Suplemento, Série I-A de 1998-05-04.* Ministério da Educação.

Portugal. (2008). *Decree-Law nº 75/08, 22 April. Diário da República n.º 79/2008, Série I de 2008-04-22.* Ministério da Educação.

Portugal/DGEEC. (2018). *Estatísticas da Educação 2017/2018.* Direção Geral de Estatísticas da Educação e Ciência.

Ryan, J. (1998). Critical leadership for education in a postmodern world: Emancipation, resistance and communal action. *International Journal of Leadership in Education, 1*(3), 257–278.

Saleiro, H. (2013). *Diretores e Lideranças: perfis em contexto escolar* (Dissertação de Mestrado). ISCTE, Instituto Universitário de Lisboa.

Santos, B. S. (2012). *Portugal: Ensaio contra a autoflagelação.* Almedina.

Shamir, B. (2011). Leadership takes time: Some implications of (not) taking time seriously in leadership research. *The Leadership Quarterly, 22*(2), 307–315.

Silva, G. R., & Sá, V. (2017). O Diretor Escolar em Portugal: formação e perfil profissional. *Espaço do Currículo, 10*(1), 62–81.

Silva, H. A. de M. (2017). *A preparação do Diretor de escola pública em Portugal Continental* (Tese de doutoramento). Faculdade de Ciências e Tecnologia, Universidade Nova de Lisboa.

Streeck, W. (2016). The rise of the European consolidation state. In H. Magara (Ed.), *Policy change under new democratic capitalism* (pp. 39–58). Routledge.

Torres, L. L. (2008). Modos de regulação cultural nas organizações escolares: um estudo sobre os perfis de liderança numa escola secundária. *Revista da Educação, XVI*(1), 77–96.

Torres, L. L., & Palhares, J. A. (2009). Estilos de liderança e escola democrática. *Revista Lusófona de Educação, 14*, 77–99.

Tuytens, M., & Devos, G. (2010). The influence of school leadership on teachers' perception of teacher evaluation policy. *Educational Studies, 36*(5), 521–536.

Tuytens, M., & Devos, G. (2011). Stimulating professional learning through teacher evaluation: An impossible task for the school leader? *Teaching and Teacher Education, 27*(5), 891–899.

Valencia, R. R. (2010). *Dismantling contemporary deficit thinking (The critical educator)*. Routledge.

Van Vossole, J. (2014). *Framing PIGS to clean their own stable*. Paper presented at the 7th ECPR General Conference. http://hdl.handle.net/1854/LU-4215403

Van Vossole, J. (2016). Framing PIGS: Patterns of racism and neocolonialism in the Euro crisis. *Patterns of Prejudice, 50*(1), 1–20.

Vekeman, E., Devos, G., & Tuytens, M. (2015). The influence of teachers' expectations on principals' implementation of a new teacher evaluation policy in Flemish secondary education. *Educational Assessment Evaluation and Accountability, 27*, 129–151.

Wallerstein, I. (2002). The itinerary of world-systems analysis; Or, how to resist becoming a theory. In J. Berger & M. Zelditch Jr. (Eds.), *New directions in contemporary sociological theory* (pp. 358–376). Rowman & Littlefield Publishers.

Index

accountability 6, 32, 46, 63, 65, 83, 91, 95, 101, 136, 138, 141, 142, 148, 153
achievement gap 6, 16–18, 22, 28
Actor-Network Theory (ANT) 118–121, 127, 131
Anglo-Saxon models of educational leadership 5
assemblages 7, 8, 118–124, 126, 127
attachment 118, 121, 122, 124–132
autonomy 8, 17, 19, 20, 38, 39, 54–57, 62, 63, 65, 66, 69–72, 82, 83, 92, 95, 105, 107, 109, 113, 114, 122, 123, 125, 126, 148, 152–154

centralized education system 7, 79, 89, 91, 93
charter 101, 102
commitment 13, 18, 55, 62, 86, 88, 89, 92, 93, 103
constriction 38, 39, 42
corporate management 62
cross-cultural leadership 3
cultural contingency 3, 127
cultural situatedness of educational leadership 5, 127
cultural turn in educational leadership studies 4, 5
Cyprus 6, 7, 79, 81–87, 89–95, 139

deconstruction of leadership 1, 2
democratic values 57, 58
deontology 101, 110
difference 6, 14–16, 18, 19, 24–26, 29, 71, 86, 114, 132, 143, 145
digital governance of education 8, 118
digital turn 117, 118
distributed leadership 74

educational commodification 3
educational establishment 38
educational leadership 1, 3–9, 12, 17, 18, 31, 37, 38, 40, 80, 101, 103, 105, 108, 109, 113, 117–120, 122, 124, 126, 131, 135, 136
effectiveness 7, 8, 64, 66, 67, 69, 70, 79, 80, 90, 102, 140, 149, 154
efficiency 8, 9, 17, 64, 66, 67, 102, 103, 122, 140

equity 6, 12, 15, 17, 18, 20–22, 32, 44

Foucault 41, 118–121, 127, 131

globalization 3, 13, 16
govern without government 64
governmentality 38, 42, 48, 63

heroic leader 3
higher education 20, 47, 101, 102, 104, 107, 112–114

inclusion 6, 13, 14, 17, 18, 21, 23, 26, 27, 32, 86, 149
indigenous models of leadership and management 4
Italy 7, 8, 117, 118, 122, 124, 127, 131, 138

leader centrism 2
leadership 3, 4, 6, 7, 8, 17, 18, 23, 28, 31, 33, 48, 51, 52, 68, 73, 74, 79–82, 84–86, 89, 90, 93–96, 120–122, 124, 127, 135–137, 140–142, 148, 155
leadership characteristics 80, 84, 85, 94–96
leadership discourses 3
Leadership for Learning 74, 137, 142
leadership for social justice 6, 17, 18, 23, 28, 31, 33, 73, 74

Malta 6, 12, 19–22
marginalization 111
McDonaldization 7, 67
Mediterranean Basin 1–3, 5, 9
models of organization 38, 39, 56, 68
multiculturalism 33

neoliberal governance 63
neoliberal governmentality 63
networked leadership 7, 86, 87
New Public Administration 68, 71–73, 138
New Public Management (NPM) 7, 64, 95, 117, 118, 122, 139

organizational authority 101

pedagogic leadership 62, 73, 74
pedagogy 47, 67, 106, 108, 112

people-centered leadership 7, 86, 88
performance 5, 15, 17, 38–40, 42, 43, 49, 59, 64, 66, 70, 91, 93, 103, 107, 111, 119, 122, 123, 125, 126, 140
performativity 15, 17, 101, 121, 135, 138, 139, 142, 153
personal attributes 7, 89, 93, 95
policy borrowing 13, 16
policy discourses 25, 30
professional attributes 90, 92, 93

reform 3, 6, 9, 12, 15, 17, 19–21, 23, 25, 27, 32, 41, 46, 47, 70, 72, 91, 101–114, 117, 118, 122, 123, 125, 126, 142, 148, 151, 152, 154
regimes of practices 8, 17
responsibility 14, 41, 43, 47, 49–52, 55, 58, 59, 62, 63, 70–74, 83, 91, 102, 103, 107, 110, 122, 140

school leader presences 126
school leader subjectivations 118–122, 131
school leaders 7, 8, 12, 19, 27, 32, 33, 80, 81, 83–96, 118, 122, 124, 125, 127, 131, 132, 137
school leadership 4, 7, 8, 17, 18, 48, 51, 52, 68, 79–82, 84–86, 89, 90, 93–96, 120–122, 124, 127, 135–137, 140–142, 148, 155

schools 4, 7, 8, 11–24, 26, 27, 29, 30, 32, 33, 38, 42–46, 48, 50–56, 58, 59, 63, 64, 66–72, 79–96, 114, 118–122, 124–127, 131, 135–137, 140–142, 148, 155
social justice 6, 11–14, 16–19, 21–33, 59, 73, 74
stakeholders 7, 21, 25, 28, 30, 32, 41, 80, 81, 83, 85, 86, 88–90, 92, 93, 101, 103, 106, 108, 110, 111, 113, 150, 152, 155
subjectivity 49, 50, 53, 127
successful school leaders 7, 80–82, 84–96

totalizing techniques 38

universality 3
university ethics 101, 110

values 4, 5, 7, 18, 21, 39, 44, 47, 51, 57, 58, 64, 66, 71, 73, 80, 86, 88, 89, 93, 95, 114, 131, 140, 141, 155
vision 7, 38, 41, 42, 44, 49, 51, 56, 57, 66, 69, 73, 74, 84, 86, 88, 89, 93, 108, 114, 141, 145, 147, 155

Western models of educational leadership 4

Printed in the United States
by Baker & Taylor Publisher Services